HOW I CAN BE REAL

ANSWERS FOR YOUTH SERIES

HOW I CAN BE REAL

LARRY RICHARDS

Illustrations by Charles Shaw

ZONDERVAN PUBLISHING HOUSE
OF THE ZONDERVAN CORPORATION
GRAND RAPIDS, MICHIGAN 49506

How I Can Be Real
Copyright © 1979 by The Zondervan Corporation

First published in 1968 by Moody Press, Chicago, under the title *Are You For Real?* Copyright © 1968 by Moody Bible Institute.

Zondervan Revised Edition 1979

Library of Congress Cataloging in Publication Data

Richards, Lawrence O
  How I can be real.

  (Answers for youth)
  Edition of 1968 published under title: Are you for real?
  Includes bibliographical references.
  SUMMARY: A guide to finding and being oneself based on Christian values.
  1. Youth—Religious life.   [1. Identity.
2. Christian life]   I. Shaw, Charles, 1941-.   II. Title.
BV4531.2.R45 1979   248'.83   79-20735
ISBN 0-310-38971-2

Printed in the United States of America

83   84   85   86   87   88 — 10   9   8   7   6   5

Contents

1

Be yourself

It hit Clare one night when she was on a date. "I always rambled on about nothing special just to keep the conversation moving," she says. "I never really shut up and listened. It seemed like I hated silence and avoided disclosing my real self.

"One night, on my first date with a certain fellow, I was babbling on about nothing when he said, 'Do you have trouble saying what you want to say?' This shut me up. He told me that he once had this problem, but that he realized unless we share ourselves with others, life becomes one big masquerade. You've got to be yourself."

You've got to be yourself.

Like Clare, you and I have times when life demands, "Be yourself!" But it's not as simple as it sounds. It's easy to say, "Be yourself!" But what if you're uncertain about who you are? What if you can't grab onto that real, solid "self" you're supposed to be?

Anyone who is uncertain surely has company! Many

teens are uncertain about themselves, and express their doubts in different ways.

Why do I get into lousy moods?
How can a person find himself?
Why am I doing the things I do?
What makes me so prone to temptation and putting God
    last when I know better?
I like myself. Is this wrong?
Who am I? Does how I think determine what I am?
Am I weird in the way I reason and think?
I seem to be changing all the time and I think it's hard to
    understand myself, my actions and my feelings.
How can we like ourselves if we can't even understand or
    cope with ourselves?
Why do I do things? Why do I sin when I don't want to?

Of course, not many teens wander through school all day with a puzzled look, asking their friends, "Who am I?" Most of the time questions like these drift below the surface. But now and then the questions come to the top.

Thoughts of the future forced Ann, a seventeen-year-old British Columbian to ask questions about herself. She writes,

> I want to become a missionary nurse. I feel that the Lord has called me to be this and I feel He has told me what field He wants me in. However, I failed ninth grade and I am not doing well in mathematics or science. How do you account for this? Is the Lord trying to show me that He doesn't want me to be a nurse?

As the self-image of "Missionary Nurse Ann" begins to shatter under the hard reality of her academic limitations, Ann is forced to ask, "If I'm not the missionary nurse I've always thought, who am I?"

Many of us even when we try to be ourselves feel the person who comes through isn't the "real me." Secular and Christian researchers agree that older teens often feel a need to discover their real selves. One researcher, who surveyed several thousand Christian high school students, discovered that *many* "are self-critical and unhappy because they feel they don't measure up to what they ought to be." He concludes that older youth "need better self-understanding—help to know the confidence and joy of which the Scriptures speak."[1]

It may be reassuring to know uncertainty about the "real you" is normal. Especially if you wonder if you're the only one with the problem. But normal or not, self-doubt is painful. It can hurt.

False fronts?

But it hurts even more to try to avoid being yourself, even though there are popular ways to dodge being honest and real.

Jack, a seventeen-year-old Michigan high schooler tried the dodge of conformity. He put up a false front and tried to pretend to be just like his friends. "Before I got into high school, I didn't smoke, swear, or drink. Now I do all three, although I don't make them a habit. I do these things because my 'friends' do. I could resist these temptations, but why don't I?"

Jack didn't want to do things he believed were wrong. But he did. To fit in, he put on a false front, and hid his real feelings behind it. The result was only a sense of failure and frustration.

There are many reasons for putting on false fronts. When I went to college I'd had few dates. Because underneath I doubted that I was important enough to be of interest, I tried to be someone else who would be more interesting. I developed a fantastic tale of a trip to Africa in search of an aardvark without teeth, backed up with all sorts of details gleaned from an encyclopedia.

This is a dangerous front. No one can be someone else, and it's hard to put on an act all the time. Underneath there's always the nagging worry of whether you'll slip and someone will find out what you're really like. Of course, a person *can* be a phony all his life. But who wants to?

There's another way to avoid the pain of learning to be yourself. Here's how Don, a twenty-year-old Pennsylvania college student, justifies his refusal to come out in the open with other people:

> I tend to be very meditative and melancholic. When placed in a social environment I can put on a good front, not showing my true nature. My greatest problem, however, is dealing with women. I keep telling myself that I

have no confidence because I have no car, nor money, nor time (being a student and working at the same time). But when summer comes I have plenty of time and money. Contrary to what I am told, I used to say that I am ugly. But I'm afraid that's no excuse now. At this point, I am putting on an anti-female front, saying that they only ruin your life!

I think that my real problem lies in the fact that I would be at a loss as to hiding my melancholic nature, and would do more thinking than speaking—and everything would remain impersonal, which is my greatest fear. Likewise, I tremble at the thought of a girl, or anyone, discovering my sensitive, overemotional nature.

What's Don doing? He's hiding behind an unreal picture of himself. He used to think he was ugly. This gave him a reason for his feelings about himself. Now that excuse is gone, so he hunts for others—no car, no money, no time. Why does Don work so hard to keep away from others? Because Don's picture of himself needs props. It won't stand up under honest evaluation.

Is Don really so sensitive and emotional that no one can understand or care for him? Other people are sensitive too. Other people care deeply. Like others, Don is a human being, capable of loving and being loved. He just isn't as different as he wants to think.

Trying to fool *yourself* is the most dangerous dodge of all. Why? Because a person tries to be what he thinks he is. Don's picture of himself isn't accurate, but accurate or not, Don *feels* fearful, sensitive, overemotional. Don's feelings and his ideas about himself have cut him off from others. They've squeezed him in on himself, and brought deepening unhappiness. This is a tragedy, for God "does not want you to be afraid of people, but to be wise and strong, and to love them and enjoy being with them"

(2 Tim. 1:7). Don's distorted picture of himself cripples him as a person and as a Christian. Don, Jack, all of us, need to be ourselves. Our real selves.

Break out to reality

What does it mean for a person to be "for real," or his or her "real self"?

First, a person needs to clear away the clutter of fuzzy ideas about himself he has collected over the years. Paul wrote to the Romans, "As God's messenger I give each of you God's warning: be honest in your estimate of yourselves" (Rom. 12:3a). This is basic.

Second, a person needs to toss away the false fronts. Paul knew about this too. He wrote, "Do things in such a way that everyone can see you are honest clear through" (Rom. 12:17b). Learning to live without false fronts isn't as hard as you may think!

We could stop with these two. Anyone who accomplished these goals would break out into reality: he would be "for real." But there's a third goal necessary for anyone who wants to be a for-real *Christian* person. Paul pinpoints it: "Lovingly follow the truth at all times—speaking truly, dealing truly, living truly—*and so become more and more in every way like Christ* who is the head of his body, the church" (Eph. 4:15).

A Christian isn't just another person. There's a new dimension to his life, a resurrection dimension. The living Jesus Christ is present inside, eager for the Christian to grow until he becomes what every Christian is destined to be—like Christ in every way! So the Christian who wants to be "for real" has to do more than to just be himself. He needs to let God break loose inside to shape and control his life. Only then will he find reality.

It's a great life when it's based on reality. You can "be a

new and different person with a fresh newness in all you do and think" (Rom. 12:2). So come along. And break out into reality.

Steps to take

Here are things you can do to apply some of the ideas in this chapter to your own life. Take these steps and the others suggested with each chapter and you *will* move closer to finding and being your real self.

1. Do you ever feel uncertain or uncomfortable about being your "real self"? Write a paragraph about your feelings or how you try to handle them.

2. Just what do you want the Lord to do for you as you work through this book? Jot down your personal goals. And begin now to pray about them.

2

Stand up!

There it was. The last buzzer—"liberty bell" they called it at Hobart High—and the kids were tumbling out of class into the wide central hall. *Upstream all the way,* Dave thought, as he pushed against the flow from study hall. *They* would *put my locker on the other end, so I have to push through the herd.*

The herd, freed and ready for it, wasn't paying much attention to Dave. There were too many other things now that the day was over.

"So I said to Ann. . . ."

"And when that jerk George struck out on his fast ball. . . . It was a curve . . . naw, it was a fast ball, high inside. George never could hit an inside. . . ."

"So what if Mrs. Jones did say to do it over, Carrie did just as bad and she never. . . ."

"Dave." A new voice cut through the tumult. "Dave, just a minute."

Oh, oh. What is it now? "Sure, Mr. Clark. Let me put my books in my locker, and I'll be right back."

15

Dave pushed harder now, anxious to get away from Mr. Clark. He could feel his stomach tighten up, and the sweat started coming right in the center of his back where it always did when something went wrong. How did Clark ever find out he'd copied his brother's college paper on delinquency?

If only he'd had more time, he might have done it himself. But there was so much to do, and how could he do anything better than Ted's anyway? Now the sweat started on the back of his neck.

These dumb kids, Dave thought, pushing against a smaller figure in

front of him. *Who gave them the whole hall?*

"Hey, Dave." Rod Grey's beefy hand pulled him around, and he faced his grinning locker-mate. "What's Clinker Clark want with you?"

"Beats me." Dave struggled to smile and look casual. Rod always gave him a hard time, anyway. *You don't suppose—no. What could Rod know? That stinkin' wise grin of his—*

"Clark's got a rep to live up to, Davie. He chews up at least one guy a week. I'm glad it's you that's goin' to fill his quota."

"Oh, I don't know. I heard he was looking for someone to tutor a muscle-bound football player. So I may see you sooner than you think, strong man."

That put him down! Now, a grin and a casual wave, then brisk steps back down the hall. Dave glanced back and grinned a little inside. *I really lit one that time. You could almost see Rod fume. These big guys. Lotsa muscle, but it's the old brain that counts.*

Out of sight, Rod wasn't much comfort. There was Clark to face. And how do you talk yourself out of a paper you copied word for word?

The sweat was still there when Dave knocked on the door. Now he could feel it on his forehead and running down his right cheek.

"Come in, Dave."

"Thanks, Mr. Clark." Dave sat in the chair where Mr. Clark motioned him.

"Here, Dave, wipe off some of that sweat. You must be warm-blooded, to perspire in an air-conditioned school."

Dave took a kleenex from the box Mr. Clark pushed toward him. *Playing cat and mouse with me.* "Yes, sir. I thought you might want to leave, so I hurried."

Mr. Clark took that one without too much reaction.

Maybe he looked just a little surprised and pleased?

"It's about your paper, Dave."

"Yes sir. I thought it might be." *Phooey. That sweat again.* Mr. Clark fumbled through some papers on his desk and finally came up with several typewritten sheets.

Here it comes! Maybe—

"Dave, I wonder if you know just what you've got here?"

"Sir?"

"This is probably the best social studies paper a high schooler has ever written for me. It's exceptional. You seem very sensitive to people, and express yourself very well. And you've done a lot of independent research."

"Well, as much as I could. There wasn't a lot of time—"

"How did you get some of these books?"

"My brother. Er, some of his college books were home, and I used them." *Oops. That was a goof!*

"Dave, what are you planning to study in college?"

"College? Oh, I don't know. I've thought about being a doctor. Guess that's what my folks expect. I've said that, anyway." Man! The knot loosened up. *I'm going to get away with it after all!*

"I don't want to influence you if you've made up your mind," Mr. Clark was going on, "but have you ever thought of a career in social work? Or teaching in the social sciences? Today the world's biggest problems are in helping people learn to live fruitful and happy lives. The physical sciences have opened prospects of wealth and leisure beyond our imaginations. But we have to equip people, people in our country and around the world, to use these benefits wisely. This is the challenge of your generation, Dave, and I think you might play a significant role in meeting it."

There was something about Mr. Clark as he talked that

Dave hadn't seen in the classroom. A warmth. An intensity of feeling. It was an exciting idea—to sort of shape people for a whole new way of life.

"As I said, Dave, this paper shows real promise. I've noticed you in class before, but this says you've got that sensitivity I mentioned. This is the key thing, sensitivity."

"It does sound interesting, Mr. Clark. I never did think of it quite that way."

"Why not think on it some more, Dave. A person has to have some meaningful purpose in life. That's what sets men apart. We can live by reason and purpose, not just by instinct."

"I guess that is important, isn't it?" *Yeah. A real solid purpose in life. And exciting. That idea of shaping people— maybe even that meathead Rod.* That brought a grin.

"Dave." Mr. Clark stood up as Dave grinned over the throught of shaping Rod. "Here's a book you might like to look at. It's called *Reconstruction of Society*. Bring it back when you're done and we'll talk some more."

"Thanks, Mr. Clark." Dave stood too, and took the book. "I *will* read it. And I would like to talk to you some more about social work."

"Good Dave. If you like, maybe we can take some Saturday and visit some projects I know of in Center City."

"Yeah. That would be great!"

It did sound good, this life-with-a-purpose bit. And fitting people for a new world. Dave grinned. The sweat was gone now. The book was light as a feather, especially with his returned paper folded in its center.

The wide hall was empty now, scuffed by the feet of hundreds of kids he might one day help shape. *Who knows?* he thought. *Anything could happen.*

* * *

"Karen, Dave's here again."
"OK, Mom. Send him on down."
"Karen, you come up."
"Oh, Mother—"
"Karen!"

Karen's dad paused and turned down the power on the mower. His soaked undershirt clung tightly to the rolls of fat that bulged out under his ribs and widened toward his belly. He wiped the sweat off his forehead with a massive sunburned arm, and heaved down on the step beside Dave.

"Hot. Too hot to work. Too bad I got no son, but—" He grinned broadly, poking a wet elbow into Dave's side. "I guess you're glad we got a girl instead, eh?"

"Yes, sir, I sure am." Dave grinned back. He tried to wipe at the wet spot on his shirt unobtrusively, and slid a little down the step.

"Well, Dave, we're glad she's got sense enough to go with a nice guy like you. Lotsa these girls start going with kids from outside of church. Then a parent starts worrying. Most teens today—"

"We had a good youth program on dating only Christians last week, Mr. Brock. It was real helpful."

"That Ben's a good youth director, I guess."

"I guess so. I don't see him a lot, but the programs are always good."

Mr. Brock leaned back against the house and lowered his head into his nest of chins. "Hot. Too hot for lawn mowing. Want a coke, Dave?"

"No thanks, Mr. Brock. But I'll be glad to get you one."

Mr. Brock nodded, then called out, "Helen, give Dave a coke for me, will you?"

Dave jumped up and hurried inside, glad to get away. Helen Brock smiled and waved Dave away from the glistening bottle she took from the refrigerator. "That's all right, Dave. Karen has come up now. You go on in and see her, and I'll take this to her dad."

The outside door slammed, and Helen sat down beside her husband, resting her hand lightly on his knee as he tipped the cold drink. "He's a nice boy, Dan. I'm so glad Karen's interested in someone like Dave."

"Uh-huh." The fat man grunted and heaved himself to his feet. "Not many around these days. Always at church. Polite. We can be thankful. If it only lasts long enough to get her through these crazy teen years!"

The mower roared again as Dave dropped down on the living room rug to watch Karen.

"Whatchadoin'?"

"I *was* washing some things downstairs till you came." Karen had that cloudy, frustrated look Dave had learned to recognize since he moved to Hobart.

"Your mother again?"

"Yes, Mother again. She's so far out of it, it's sickening. Just 'cause I had a halter top on when you came, I had to come up and change. Everybody wears them today, but *my* mother—"

"Yeah." Dave nodded. A frown twitched just between his eyebrows, and he looked sympathetically at Karen.

"Oh, Dave." Impulsively Karen grabbed his hand and tears started to trickle down her cheeks. "If I didn't have you to talk to, I don't know what I'd do."

Dave squeezed a little tighter. He didn't like these moods of Karen's. But there wasn't much you could do.

She'd sniff a little, and hold his hand, and wear a long face. Times like these he couldn't talk to her—like about the invitation from Mr. Clark, or the way he'd put down Rod. But usually she came out of it. And besides, who else did he really know in Hobart? And how could he get to know anybody else? Everybody knew that he and Karen were paired off. And a guy had to have someone. Karen was talking on.

"... and every time it's a big fight. I can't talk with her; it always gets to be an argument. Like today I told her we wanted to go out to the Milk Shake, and she said I had to do my room. I live in my room, not her. Nag, nag, nag is always all I get. 'Nobody wants a sloppy housekeeper, Karen.' 'Work first then play, Karen'—

"Dave?"

Her question brought him back sharply. "Yeah?"

"You don't care, do you? I mean, there are more important things than keeping house."

"There sure are." Dave smiled, reassuringly, he hoped. "And I like you just the way you are." They both squeezed harder. It was one of those moments of complete acceptance. No faults, no blemishes, were recognized or admitted. And as long as they had each other, what did it matter?

"Listen." Dave pulled away. "I've got to go." Karen stood up too and brushed away her tears. "Sure you can't make it to the Shake?"

"No. And I don't dare sneak out. They'd kill me if I got caught."

"Friday night?"

"OK, I think so."

"Good-bye." Dave went out the back door and across the yard, and vaulted over the back fence into the alley, conscious that Karen was watching him. He wasn't a campus hero like Rod, but it didn't hurt to show a little muscle. And he didn't look at all bad. Kinda graceful.

Dave waved to Karen as he passed out of sight behind the garage. She was pretty. And he could be sort of comfortable with her. He knew what she was like. And just how to act when she was in one of her moods, or almost any time.

Maybe I am sensitive, he thought. *Maybe Mr. Clark is right and I ought to be a social worker or something. Or maybe a preacher. They have to work with people. Yeah. Who knows?*

* * *

"Don't throw your books on the chair, Dave."

Boy. That's Mom all over! Still in a good mood, Dave dropped Mr. Clark's book on the sofa and started toward the kitchen. He hesitated, turned back just long enough to slip out Ted's paper, and squeeze it carefully into his pants pocket.

"What's for supper, Mom?" She looked good, hair in a frazzled brown halo, short and a little plump, busy in the kitchen. *Just like moms are supposed to,* Dave thought. Dave pulled open the refrigerator door and selected a big red Delicious apple.

"Food, Dave, not apples. Put it back."

"Can't." Dave smiled and bit into the bright skin and juicy meat. "Too hungry."

"You'll ruin your supper." She looked up, petulant but surrendering. Like she always did.

Dave grinned again. "I can always eat more of your cooking anyway."

"Well, tonight it's only cold cuts and potato salad. Too hot to cook in here. I wish you or Dad would get up the grill for the backyard—"

"Maybe Saturday, Mom."

Dave wandered out and flopped on the sofa, picking up the sports section of the paper. A hundred-thousand-dollar bonus! Wow! Social work, phooey. If only he was a little more athletic. Like Rod. Or some of the guys on the school baseball team.

Dave's dad arrived like always—breathlessly. He burst into the house, dropped off his stuffed briefcase in the study, quickly changed into slacks and shirt, and grabbed for the sports page. "Hi, son. Give me a look, hey?"

"Sure, Dad." *Might as well give in on that one!* he thought. *Besides—*

"Dad."

"Uh-huh."

"I had a talk with Mr. Clark today. He thinks I've got talent for social work and social science. Says I'm sensitive to people."

"That's good."

"Think I might go with him some Saturday to see how people do it. He gave me a book too."

Behind the paper, Dad's head bobbed his interest. "Thought you planned to be a doctor, Dave."

"Yeah. But maybe I ought to be a social worker. It's pretty important too."

"Well, whatever you want. Important thing is to do something worthwhile. And be a Christian at it. You know—" Down came the paper. "I was talking to Lieutenant Briggs today. He was telling me all about the teen vandalism these days—kids breaking windows, scratching paint on cars, tearing off aerials. I told him how you go to church regularly and never get involved in things like that. He said he's not much for religion but has to admit that kids in our church aren't the ones he has trouble with.

"Dave, you can find chances for witness like that in any job. Doctor *or* social work."

"Yeah." Dave's dad was submerged in the paper again before his "yeah" got out. After a while Dave got up and took the book to his room and began to read. *Reconstruction of Society.*

> The increased pace of life in our modern, mobile society has multiplied immeasurably the factors tending toward the disintegration of that society. Impersonality, which is fostered by the fragmentation of the life of modern man into isolated compartments of job, home, social, recreational, and religious life, seems both to be the goal and the ultimate destroyer of the individual. Lost in a sea of faces, all blandly set to cut off any depth-relationship with others, modern man seeks anonymity and with it finds isolation from the values which a community must hold in common to. . . .

Wow! What in the world? Dave thought. *Back to the old sports page! Do you suppose all social scientists talk like that?*

"Dave! Supper."

Dave sloshed some water over his hands, running the faucet loudly enough for Mom to hear, and thumped downstairs.

"Herbert, you're the only man I ever saw who could eat faster than Dave!" Mom's private war on wolfed food was on again.

"Got to, hon. Trustee meeting at 7:30. Dave, tell your mother about your talk with Mr. Clark." Dad always was a master at misdirection!

"Who's Mr. Clark, Dave?"

"He's my social science teacher. Gave me an A+ on a term project, and said I ought to go into social work. Said I was sensitive."

"Where's the paper, Dave?" Dad wiped his mouth and pushed back his chair. "I'd like to show it to Lieutenant

Briggs. Let him know all teens aren't delinquents."

"Er, Mr. Clark kept it." The words came easily now, smoothly. "I think he wants to show it to some other classes." *They might not remember Ted's paper. But—*

"Maybe I'll call him, Dave. I'd like to have it for Briggs."

"Please, Dad!" The edge on Dave's voice stopped his dad as he shrugged into a light sports coat. "Don't. I—I don't want Mr. Clark to think I was bragging or anything."

"Well, Dave, don't get too modest." Dad clapped him on the shoulder and turned away toward the door. "Besides, I'm the one who's being proud, not you."

The door slammed, and Dave could hear his dad striding down the drive, whistling as he got into the car and gunned the motor.

That blew it! *Blast Dad, anyway. Always so cheerful. Just go ahead and do it his way, no matter what.*

Dave got up suddenly, almost tipping over his chair.

"Why, what's the matter, Dave?"

"Nothing. Just gotta go."

"Where are you going tonight?"

"Milk Shake. Karen and I made a date." He was almost out the door.

"Dave! In those clothes?"

"It's all right, Mom. They're clean." That always got her. They're clean. The door slammed as Dave ran down the walk. He kicked a rock viciously, and felt a little better when it caromed off the fence with a loud clatter.

Well, it would work out. Dad would probably forget anyway. He only brought it up to get Mom off his back. But it sure was a terrible thing to have hanging over a guy's head.

A few houses down the street Dave took the folded

theme out of his pocket and carefully shredded it into a garbage can awaiting the morning pickup. Good-bye, good-bye, good-bye. And a good good-bye!

* * *

Dave found Ken and his crew where he expected, down by Mickey's bowling alley. They were leaning against the wall, not really doing anything, but just being there.

"Anything tonight?" Dave knew, of course, that they were the ones. All the kids knew. But nobody said anything.

Ken shook his head. "Too hot."

Dave wasn't sure if Ken meant the weather or the police. It *was* hot. He leaned against the building, felt its rough face through his thin shirt. The bricks were still warm, warmer than the air. His back started to prickle with tiny droplets of sweat as the building heat soaked into his muscles. It felt good. Relaxing.

One of Ken's crew shied a stone across the street, earning a dirty look from a bypasser. He stared right back, deliberately picked up another stone, and threw it. The bypasser, an overdressed woman of about fifty, stuck her nose up in the evening air and hurried on.

"Old bag!"

Dave pushed back a little into the shadow as the woman shot a look back at the stone thrower and was rewarded with a loud repeat. "Old bag!"

The fellows laughed. And Dave laughed too. She sure did look shook. Like she hated the teens and hated not being able to do anything about them. And—he giggled a little—she really was an old bag.

"Come on, guys." Ken pushed away from the wall and turned down the street. "Let's go do something."

Dave hung back. But when Ken looked toward him, he

pushed out too. "Yeah. Might as well." *Why not? Why not stick with them for a little while?* he thought. *I sure wouldn't be welcomed by the old bag and her kind.*

"What's to do?" The conversation came in leisurely spurts, almost timed to their slow pace. Twenty steps, then—

"Not much. Too early."

Twenty more.

"Could get some beer at Benny's."

Twenty more.

"Too far."

Everybody, thought Dave, *is in a hurry but us. Dad hurries to work or to church; Clark hustles us into college; Karen's hot to be her own boss right away. Hurry, hurry, hurry. All but us.*

"I got an idea!"

Twenty steps.

"Yeah?"

"Let's follow some dame home after the movie lets out. Just walk behind her. I bet it'd scare her to death."

"Hey!" The small group stopped, a little excited now. "We never tried it, but that's got real possibilities!"

"How about you?" Ken turned to Dave, and all eyes switched to his face. He suddenly felt lit up, there in the shadows. Like there was a spotlight on his face.

"Yeah. Sure." He was in now. Might as well make the plunge. "We did it a couple times in Mead when I lived there. Why, the cops even put on a special patrol, the skirts were so scared."

He had them now.

"How? How'd ya work it?"

"Well—" Dave thought fast. "We only had one guy follow at a time. Too easy to trace a gang. And besides, when we had three or four followin' in different parts of town, we just about drove the cops crazy."

"Smart." It was Ken himself, nodding.

"And we got a trademark. We all whistled, real low. A weird tune. It scared 'em twice as bad, and it made the cops think there was just one guy doing it." It was building now. One idea suggested another, and soon Dave's tale was fitted with the kind of detail that spelled reality. "And we had one thing for sure. If anybody got caught, he was to take the whole rap. No one was to rat on the others. That's the most important thing."

"Did anybody get caught?"

"Yeah, finally. He took the rap though, and they put him in the nut factory for three months. Then he got out, and nobody was the wiser."

"Man, let's go!"

"Yeah!"

No twenty steps between comments now. The gang was excited, and Dave was excited too. It was really something, this being looked up to by all the fellows. Why, Ken's crew was just about his own. Dave's crew. Sounded kinda good. Sensitive, that was the word. Be sensitive, and you can mold people.

"Dave." It was Ken's voice. "You show us how."

"Yeah."

"Yeah, Dave."

"Show us how."

She was about half a block in front of him now. Dave swung in behind and started walking slowly, pacing her.

Hunch up. Make your right shoulder a little higher than your left. And shuffle your feet. Louder.

There! She's heard.

A sort of tingle played over Dave's spine as he watched her quicken her pace. He matched it, drawing a little closer now with his loud, shuffling walk.

You could see her back stiffen, shoulders pull together. And her neck. It seemed to get longer, tighter. Why, she was afraid to turn around. Afraid to look.

Try the whistle. Make it low. A little louder, but slow. Weird.

Dave knew Ken was watching, hanging in the shadows down and across the block. A little faster. His own heart was pounding faster; he could feel the excitement of the primitive tingling along his nerves.

Closer. *How long before she'll break?*

Closer. *Don't look back!*

Closer. *Whistle.*

There!

With a little gasp, she bolted up the steps of the nearest house and pounded on the door, pressing against the wood, her sobs coming loud and broken. The porch light flashed on.

Caught in its brilliance, Dave slipped quickly behind a tree, then bent and ran along its shadow across the street and back to the welcomed darkness.

They found him. They crowded around, patting him on the back, making admiring remarks.

"Hey, let's do it again!"

"Yeah, it's my turn!"

"No." Dave was surprised at the firmness in his voice. "No, it's better to wait a couple of nights. Even three. You got to build it slow for the biggest effect."

They nodded. They followed him. Dave swelled inside but played it careful, cool.

"Let's go celebrate."

"All right." It was Ken, trying to regain control. "Let's hook a car and go to Benny's for beer. It's late enough."

"OK," said Dave, "I'll drive."

The car Dave drove stank with beer. Its stale smell choked him, its revolting yeastiness fouled the back of his mouth and it seemed to seethe sickeningly in his stomach. *One stinking can! Ugh!*

Dave rolled down the car window and leaned out, letting the whistling air force its way into his nose and mouth. Still that awful taste and smell.

Dave glanced toward Ken. His head was tipped back, draining one can, a six-pack nestled on his lap. The other fellows were guzzling too. How can they stand it?

Maybe a little faster.

"That's it, Dave. Go!"

"Ride it." Ken was laughing, pointing up the road. "Hit that curve at fifty. I did it the other night."

Dave pushed down. *Hit it? Fifty? Fifty-five!*

The car rocketed around the curve, struggling on two wheels before it dropped back.

"Hit it, man."

"Go, go, go!"

Yeah. Hit it, and go. This part you could make at sixty, easy. Dave gunned down again, but the stolen car skidded on a patch of oil and spun out of control.

Jamming hard on the brakes as the wheel tore itself out of his hands, Dave caught just a glimpse of a face in a passing car as they skidded by it, into a mesh fence, and bounced back across the highway into a telephone pole.

Karen!

* * *

"Dave!" His dad shook him, pulling him up out of sleep. "Dave. Come on, get up."

"Whatsamatter?" His mind struggled, refusing to come out of its stupor.

"Dave, it's the police. They think you can help them."

Police! Dave was awake now. Really awake!

"I just got a call from Lieutenant Briggs. He thinks you and Karen were witnesses to an accident involving a stolen car.

"But Dad—"

"They traced Karen, and her folks said you were out together. You know, you should have gone down and reported the accident yourself. Here." Dad passed a pair of pants and a clean shirt at Dave, then dashed out of the room.

Dave looked at the clock. *Four o'clock. Dash, dash, dash. Even at 4:00 A.M.*

It was a quiet ride. Dave ducked his head and pretended to doze. He didn't want to talk to Dad or anybody. His head hurt. His stomach still rebelled against the beer, and now it was beginning to knot up. He could feel his arm muscles begin to twitch too. Dear God! How had he gotten into this?

"Glad to meet you, Dave." Lieutenant Briggs was a big man. *Big like Rod,* Dave thought. *But he talks just like Dad, on and on.*

"Heard a lot about you from your dad. Sorry to get you up. Some kids stole a car. Hot-wired it, and drove it off from the owner's house. Maybe you know him. A teacher at your school, Clark's the name, be down here in a minute.

"We've got a good line on the kids who did it. Think it's a bunch we keep our eyes on. Nothing much till now.

"It's been a hot night." This to Dave's dad. "Some masher scared a twelve-year-old girl almost to death. Had to put her under sedation. Then this. Well. . . ."

Dave sat down on a wooden bench and pressed his back against the wall, hard, and closed his eyes.

When he opened them, Karen and her folks were there. Karen was white. She looked right at Dave, then pressed closer to her mother. She didn't speak. *She knows,* Dave thought. *She knows.*

Only Mr. Brock said anything. He glared at Dave. "Dave, if I'd have known anything like this would happen I wouldn't have changed my mind and let Karen join you."

Dave closed his eyes. Tight.

Then it was two doors, almost at once. The big front door swung in and Mr. Clark stepped through. He looked in surprise toward Dave, then questioningly at the lieutenant, who shook his head.

Ken and one of his crew were pushed by a patrolman through a side door, almost hidden behind the lieutenant's desk. Ken still looked cocky, a hard sneer on his face. But his eyes looked tight and scared as he glanced sidelong toward Dave.

"You fellows were lucky, I'd say." It was Briggs' voice. "If that fence hadn't taken the impact, you'd be dead by now. Oh, yes. We know it was you. And I think we've got someone who can identify you. Dave!"

Dave opened his eyes. They were all looking at him, all of them. His dad. Karen. Mr. Clark. Ken. All looking at him—

"Dave, stand up here."

He swallowed. He had to say something. He had to open his mouth. He—

"Dave! Stand up!"

Steps to take

1. Jot down what each person facing Dave in the police station expects him to say.

2. Why does Dave feel trapped and at a loss for words now? He has never seemed at a loss before, even when covering up something he has done wrong.

3. Do you think Dave is "for real"? Write down why or why not.

4. Dave felt his sensitivity gave him power to mold people and shape them for his purposes. Look back over his relationship with each person. Has Dave really molded others? What has he done? Think it through.

3

Mirror image

During the afternoon and evening that we followed Dave, he caught onto an important truth about himself. Dave was sensitive. He had a gift; he could read people.

But Dave didn't see the implications of his gift. To Dave this meant "ability to mold people." In his case it meant just the opposite: Dave was molded. Sensing what others thought of him, *Dave tried to become the person they expected him to be!*

Mr. Clark saw Dave as a sensitive, talented young person suited for social work. So Dave started to play the role. Dave even fooled himself. He felt he *was* the kind of person Mr. Clark pictured—dedicated, sensitive, purposeful.

Karen's dad and mom thought Dave was a nice, polite, sincere Christian young person. So Dave talked of the church youth program, and thoughtfully asked if he could get Mr. Brock a coke.

To Karen, Dave was a sympathetic, trusted companion, who understood her and accepted her. Dave didn't like

Karen's moodiness, but he never showed it. He frowned sympathetically on cue; he reached "impulsively" for her hand; he said just the right things. He became what she wanted him to be.

At home Dave was more relaxed, but he still played a part. The sudden request to see his term paper almost threw him. But how quickly Dave slipped into an acceptable role; he became the shy, humble son who didn't want to brag!

With Ken's crew Dave became the budding hood. The same polite boy Mr. Brock knew, laughed at the "old bag." More important, he actually *felt* "old bag!" When Dave almost took over Ken's crew that night, it wasn't because he was leading them. It was because he sensed where they were going and quickly followed *their* lead! Sensitive Dave let others mold *him.*

Dave was like a compass needle, and other people were like magnets. With Mr. Clark, Dave swung over and reflected his ideas. With Karen he reflected hers. At home he swung to harmonize with his parents, and with the boys he was like them.

Why was Dave so frustrated in the police station? Partly because of the trouble he was in, but only partly. He felt so lost largely because he faced four strong personalities, *each of whom expected him to be someone different!* Like a compass placed in the center of four magnets, his personality needle went crazy. He couldn't fit all four pictures. He was lost.

Figure 1

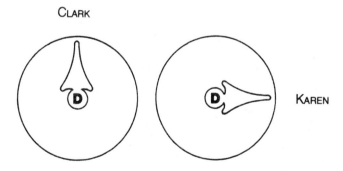

Dave could shift his personality to fit each person's picture of him.

When you look at Dave like this you realize a tragic truth. Dave seems able to get along in almost every situation, but deep down there in the center where *he* is, there's nothing. Dave is a flat zero. Dave isn't for real.

Who is Dave?

Dave is a "pure" example of what some psychologists call an *expedient* personality—a person who changes to fit any situation. You probably call a person like this something else. Take a man in your church who prays loudly in prayer meetings yet is unethical in business and shares dirty jokes at out-of-town conventions. Your word for him? Hypocrite. Next time say it sadly. Of all men he's most to be pitied. He's a nothing.

Figure 2

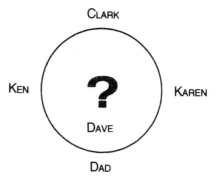

What could Dave do when he had to fit into four **different** roles at the same time?

But Dave is something more to us than an expedient personality. He's an illustration. When he reflects what others see in him, he shows us something of the way all personalities are formed. This reflective process—seeing ourselves the way others see us—is a big part of the way everyone's "self" is shaped. But by the time a person reaches the later teen years he should be struggling to get above this level of living—this situation in which "you" are simply a mirror image of what others think you are.

Two things make this struggle particularly difficult. One: the reflective process isn't conscious. We're usually no more aware than Dave was when we act according to someone else's direction. We tend to accept the pictures others have of us without stopping to ask: Say! Is this really *me?* Are they right when they say I'm not smart enough for college? Or too irresponsible to take on this project? Or too hotheaded to control myself?

When we unthinkingly buy a picture like one of these, something else happens. We *act* to fit the picture. After all, if I *am* too hotheaded to control myself, why try to hold back when I get mad? And then when I lose control my actions "prove" that the picture was true.

Life moves round and round in cycles like this (see Figure 3). We get a picture of ourselves, act to fit it, and thus strengthen the picture. In this way we build into our personality various ideas of "me." *Yet, such pictures are not necessarily true.* We are not caught, helplessly slaves of what we think we're like today. We don't have to be molded!

There's a second difficulty: The pictures we get of ourselves are reflected by cloudy mirrors at best, and often warped ones. A mother with an unwanted child often reflects a picture that says, "You are unlovely. Unwanted. A burden." And the person grows up feeling worthless.

Figure 3
How do we build ideas of ourselves?

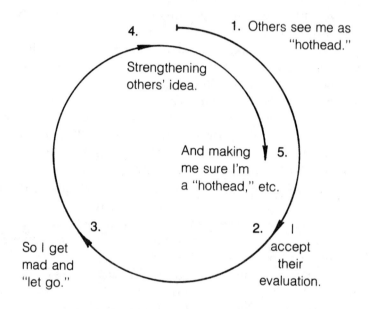

Or a dad tries to make his son the athlete he never was. He spends hours with the boy, training him to hit a baseball or throw a football. Yet, because some fellows mature later than others, this boy never becomes a star.

To the father he's a failure. And this picture is reflected. The son, sensing his dad's evaluation, accepts it as accurate. No use trying then. He believes he has no chance, no future. He's typed himself as a failure.

Pictures like these are distorted. To God (and ultimately His evaluation is the one that counts) each of us is of infinite worth. Christ cared enough to die for us. And each has a unique place in God's plan. God sees each Christian as someone who "in his own special way" can help others so that we will all be healthy and growing and full of love (see Eph. 4:16). There need be no "failures." There is a purpose in your life, a place only you can fill.

Yet, because the influence of others is so powerful, a warped picture may be accepted. And life can be forced into a tragic pattern that does not need to be.

Bust the mirrors!

While the reflective process may cause problems, it is a necessary element of personality growth. The big challenge is to understand the process and how it helps or hinders in the struggle to become real persons.

And that is the purpose of this chapter—to sketch quickly how persons grow (*the process*), and to focus on one by-product formed in persons who get dropped in front of warped mirrors (*the problem*).

The process. We can visualize it in three steps (shown in Figure 4). The process starts way back in babyhood with learning (unconsciously) to fit in with others. Maybe we grabbed the cereal spoon and slopped applesauce on dad. And got popped—a slap on the hand and a firm "No, no, no!" We probably got him again, but before long we had the idea. Spoons are for eating, not decorating parents.

If we were slow talkers, mom and dad may have developed another strategy. They simply paid no attention to hands waved toward the bread dish, or tears shed in front of the TV, until we used the word for the thing we wanted. Not much was said to us about talking, but again we got the idea. We learned to fit in with their expectations.

Figure 4
How are personalities formed?

1. We learn to fit others' expectations.

2. We imitate "pattern" people.

3. We decide for ourselves by applying self-chosen principles.

This doesn't mean that a child is simply a bundle of formless wax whom parents shape at will. We are born with individual differences—big differences. But even the differences are subject to shaping. Take two young children, both born with built-in wiggles. To one set of parents, activity means badness, bother. Their child senses their feelings, tries to conform, but has a tough time. He may rebel and be himself at the price of being labeled "bad." Or he may learn to control himself and hide his feelings and desires. Parents of the other wiggler may view this trait as desirable. "This kids' going to be a real althlete," a dad may say delightedly of his three-year-old. Thus they channel their child's natural activity and form his feelings about himself.

The main thing is, it's by sensing the parents' viewpoint that the child's behavior patterns are formed. When my cousin was three he staggered out of bed one night and headed for the bathroom. Half asleep, he didn't quite make it. But he thought he had. Actually he only got to the living room door, where the sight of him carefully using his nonexistent toilet completely broke up my aunt and uncle. He awoke to their roars of laughter.

A few nights later they had company. Well, you guessed it. Out he marched to the living room door and, wide awake, repeated his performance. The poor kid couldn't understand his folks' reaction this time. It just wasn't the same!

See the point? No one had praised him. But his parents' reaction had seemed to say that what he had done was entertaining. Reading their laughter as approval, he was motivated to do it again.

We expect children to do things just to gain approval. But it's sad when older youth do it too. Yet, more than one study has shown that it happens—regularly. Most teens are "far more sensitive to what others think than to any 'voice from within.' " They're hung up in childhood, denying themselves and their beliefs, to fit in. They are squelching their real selves, not being for real, and we can get beyond that.

A second major factor in the early shaping process is imitation. We tend to pattern ourselves after others. This process also is unconscious. We don't *decide* to be like dad; we just start to fit our personality to his. Usually, by the way, it is mom or dad we imitate. Even the things that we don't particularly like—that nasty habit of yelling when they want to get us on the move—seem to seep into our own personality.

A recent study of college freshmen pointed up how large a role such patterning plays. Freshman students were asked to list people they saw as most important in their lives: a parent, a teacher, etc. Next they rated them-

selves on a personality profile, using twenty-five characteristics like those shown in Figure 5. Finally they rated
the people they had listed on the same scale. The results?
High school graduates just leaving home tend to see
themselves very like their parent. If one sees dad as warm,
he feels that he too is warm. If dad is hardworking, he
views himself as hardworking too. Imitation plays a big
part in shaping personalities!

Figure 5
The type of categories used on the college personality-profile
study

	1	2	3	4	5	6	7	
Aggressive	—	—	—	—	—	—	—	Passive
Warm	—	—	—	—	—	—	—	Cold
Lazy	—	—	—	—	—	—	—	Hardworking

A check mark indicated the degree of each quality the college
freshmen saw in themselves and others. Separate forms were
used for each person rated.

As children grow and develop then, two major pro-
cesses shape their personalities: (1) they respond to
others' expectations and desires, and (2) they tend to imitate. The significant thing is that *both these factors operate
unconsciously*. The child doesn't *choose* to fit in. He
doesn't *choose* to imitate. He does these things without
conscious decision.

This is what divides the man from the boy, the adult
from the child. Living by choice. By decision. Here's a
high school success story shared by an eighteen-year-old
from Delaware.

I was bothered about my fruitless witnessing life during
my junior year when I discovered that I really did not have

anyone to witness to. I had become so wrapped up in church work and Campus Life that all my friends were professing Christians. In the two or three years that I had lived in the area, I had never had any unsaved classmates over to my house or ever gone over to one of their houses after school. Thus, with much prayer and guidance I found several people I would like to have known and took steps to meet them on their social level. I promised the Lord I would become friends with them for His sake.

After three months of my senior year, one person seemed to be singled out by circumstances. I spent many tense moments trying to break the ice just to be friends. It was a real comfort for me to have the attitude that I was becoming a friend because I liked this person. Many times I was with him without the slightest inclination of pushing him towards a decision for Christ or stuffing him like a turkey with the Gospel. I eventually got to know him well enough to experience a rare joy in sharing Christ when before I had been afraid and even ashamed to do it. As a result, two people have come to a saving knowledge, and I feel at ease to talk about my Savior instead of cringing and stumbling through a prefabricated list of steps.

See it? He ran into a problem. He faced it, prayed about it. He saw a solution that didn't come from the folks, or from the youth group at church. It was his own. And he acted. The result was not only the salvation of two of his new friends, but he himself had become real—"at ease to talk about my Savior instead of cringing and stumbling." He's not living according to anybody's pattern—that of his Christian friends or of his unsaved classmates. This person is living by choice. He's for real. And you can be too.

The problem is this. *We can't go through the process of trying to fit in with others' expectations without soaking up some of their feelings about us.* So we slowly gain a pretty definite concept of our own worth and value from others around us.

This view isn't always accurate. Some friends of ours have four-year-old twin girls, one of whom is known as the "peacemaker." The other day they discovered the twins fighting, with one seated on top, pounding her sister vigorously and shouting angrily, "I am so the peacemaker!" Even when there is evidence to the contrary, people's feelings about themselves tend to persist!

A teen-ager who has a low opinion of his intelligence may get good grades and still feel that he's not very smart. "If I were really smart, I wouldn't have to study so hard for what I get," he says. "I was lucky." "But it was a *low* B." He can invent any number of reasons to explain away evidence. Even a high IQ score isn't likely to convince him, because his evaluation is based on feelings, not necessarily on facts.

If we're to evaluate ourselves honestly and fairly, we need to understand something of how we feel about ourselves.

How do you feel about yourself? Take the profile test on page 00 *before you read on.* Check the one space in five which most nearly expresses your reaction to each statement.

Finished? Then a word about the questions. Each one is based on research done by Morris Rosenberg, a sociologist and researcher, and serves as an indicator of the way a person feels about himself. If your check marks fell mostly to the *left* of the center column, down deep you have a low estimate of yourself. Your self-esteem is low. The farther to the left the pattern of checks lies, the stronger is your feeling. This means that you tend to downgrade yourself. You're probably smarter than you think. You're probably better looking than you think. Your feelings about yourself probably make you *undervalue* yourself and your talents.

Profile test

	Definitely	Probably	Neutral	Unlikely
1. I am terribly hurt if someone criticizes or scolds me.				
2. I find it hard to talk when I meet new people.				
3. I often feel lonely.				
4. I don't like to contribute to discussions in class at school.				
5. I doubt if I will be as successful as most people				
6. I am deeply concerned when someone has a poor opinion of me.				
7. I do not want a job that demands a lot of competition.				
8. I tend to be a rather shy person.				
9. I tend to daydream a lot.				
10. I am eager to get along with others.				

If you are going to do what we set out to do, that is, "be honest in your estimate of yourself" (Rom. 12:3), you'll have to be on your guard against this tendency.

If your checks lie to the right of the center column, deep down you have a positive picture of yourself. You probably see yourself as someone who is worthwhile, with something positive to contribute to life and to others. Your self-esteem is higher.

Of the two, it's better to feel good about yourself than to feel bad. For one thing, it's easier to be "for real" if you feel that you're worthwhile.

There's another reason why it's better to feel good about yourself. Life isn't static. We don't get stranded on a broken treadmill. Life is moving; we're moving. We'll each be different, for better or for worse, next week, next month, next year. But the person who feels negatively about himself is less likely to see the future as an adventure and an opportunity. He's apt to drag his feet. His feelings about himself can weigh him down, hold him back, and stunt his growth toward reality.

Also, the fact is, a feeling of worth-whileness is closer to the real truth. Oh, I don't mean that you're not a sinner, nor theologically and actually "bad" in God's sight. I mean that as a human being you're redeemable, no matter what your past. You're made in God's image, twisted by sin, sure, but still the pinnacle of His creation. You are the object of God's love. He doesn't think you're worthless.

Another thing. You may not (in fact) be athletic enough to be the sports hero you'd like to be. You may not (in fact) be smart enough to earn a Ph.D. But you are (in fact!) useable; you are able to contribute. There's a place in life that only you can fill, talents that equip you to help yourself and others. And that isn't being worthless. Remember this as we go on toward being a real person.

So if the quiz showed you feel negatively about yourself, watch out for a tendency to downgrade yourself. The truth is that you are worthwhile, you are important, and you can be for real. The facts, and faith, can change your feelings!

So let's summarize. Where are we on our way toward reality?

1. We've seen that a for-real person is someone who is what he seems to be. He acts the way he really is, without false fronts.

2. We've taken an in-depth look at Dave, the zero.

He isn't what he seems to be. He only acts the way others expect him to act. He's all false front.

3. We've looked at the process of responding to others that is a dominant force in shaping personality. This is part of every person's growing up.

4. We've seen that the person who is real has gotten beyond letting others' expectations rule his life. He lives by conscious choice, making his own decisions.

5. We've seen too that the shaping process forms feelings about ourselves within us. If these feelings are negative, if our self-esteem is low, they make us downgrade ourselves and can hinder our progress toward reality.

Now we're ready to go into some crucial areas, to face both the *feelings* and the *facts*. In the next chapters you'll find some practical guidelines for becoming that for-real person you want to be.

Steps to take

1. Write a brief description of yourself as your parents see you. If you wish, also write a description as your best friend sees you.

2. You may or may not feel the view others have of you is accurate. (1) If you feel the descriptions *are* accurate, give them to your folks and friend. Ask if this is really the way they see you. (2) If you feel their view of you is inaccurate, try to decide *why* they have a false picture.

3. If on the basis of the quiz on page 47 you seem likely to have a lower opinion of yourself than you should, make a list of *evidence* on which you can evaluate your strong and weak points.

4

It only hurts for a little while

Miss Giles was nervous. *If only Jack were more dependable,* she thought, glancing around the room all prepared now for her junior high youth group's yearly parents' program.

She couldn't help liking Jack, a big, strapping four-teen-year-old. He had a ready grin, a wild sense of humor, an almost puppyish clumsiness. And he was intelligent, as well as a natural leader.

But Jack was also something else: undependable. Miss Giles noticed it when she took over the youth group in January. Give him a part, and he always seemed to forget. Or he'd get stubborn and refuse to do it. Or he'd start clowning, and get the whole group roaring. Twice he hadn't even bothered to show up. *No wonder I feel a little nervous,* she thought. But then that magazine article had said, "The cure for irresponsibility is responsibility." And Jack had so much potential! So—out on a limb she went and gave Jack the major part for tonight's parents' program. *Oh, dear.* She twisted uncomfortably in her chair. *I wonder where Jack is now.*

Jack, on his way to church, was feeling rotten. He hated it, and he hated his folks for making him go, and his thoughts bubbled in anger. Just for a moment, let's slip into Jack's mind, and feel with him.

Blast that awful Miss Giles! Now, why did I think that? I wish I didn't slip into thinking bad things. Why can't I keep from doing things like that?

Really, I can't do anything right. He picks up a stone and throws it at a telephone pole. *Missed! I knew I would. Some kids are good at sports, but I'm not. I'm clumsy. Can't hit a baseball. Fall over my own feet at football. Can't do anything.*

My stomach is hurting. With every step toward the church, he feels sicker. *Why didn't I look at my part this week? When that postcard came from Miss Giles to remind me, I tried. But it all looked so hard. And even if I did learn it, I knew I'd just make a big fool of myself Sunday.*

Why do I always have to blurt out some stupid thing when I get in front of the kids? Then they all laugh at me, and I feel so stupid. And then I just can't seem to stop. I grin and laugh and act stupid and silly—

There's the church.

How can Miss Giles do such an awful thing to me? She must know I can't do the part. She must hate me a lot. I can tell from the way she's been acting lately. She gets real sarcastic when I say anything in planning group on Tuesdays.

She must know I can't do the part. She's about as nasty as they come. It'll serve her right if I make a fool of myself and spoil her silly old program. It'll serve her right if I don't even stand up. No, I'm not going to stand up—not in front of all those people. And she'd better not try and make me!

Jack and Miss Giles. Two people who completely misunderstand each other—and Jack.

In the last chapter we saw some outside sources of a person's self-image or picture of himself. Looking back over the thoughts of Jack and Miss Giles, we can pinpoint another source—a physical one.

Early adolescence is a period of rapid physical change. Bodies shoot up and fill out, voices change, skin blemishes develop and disappear. And young people living in the bodies study themselves, and their ideas of what they're "really like" grow.

Note, for instance, how Miss Giles views Jack. Big,

strapping, friendly, good sense of humor, a cute clumsiness, intelligent, a natural leader. In other words, to her Jack is a young person with great talent and potential.

But Jack, inside his changing body, has another picture altogether. That "cute clumsiness" is to Jack an unbearable weight of failure. He can't hit a baseball. He falls over his feet at football. He's big in a world where "big" and "athlete" are equated; yet, he's no good at sports. Thus his very size is a source of embarrassment. When the kids laugh, it's not *with* him but *at* him. He sees himself as a buffoon, the clumsy kidder. And every laugh makes him feel more stupid and more silly.

So Jack's picture of himself controls his perception of others' actions. This is important to understand. Your physical self can color your self-evaluation and warp your insights into how others see you.

The memory lingers on

Very often young teens like Jack who spurt up suddenly simply can't coordinate well enough to hit a baseball or block an opposing football player. Before long (maybe six months, maybe two years) coordination will catch up with size. But the self-portrait formed now may linger on. Jack may continue to think of himself as inept, as stupid, as clumsy, and he may see only contempt in others' well-meant laughter or remarks.

Nearly every young teen-ager is unhappy to some degree about his body. Some feature is too outstanding. Maybe a nose, or a cluster of freckles. With me it was uncontrollable hair (my nickname for a couple of years in high school was "bushman"). It's normal to become extremely sensitive about that feature, even to feel that it's a blemish that ruins us. More than half of young teen girls are worried because they're too tall. More than half of young teen boys are worried because they're too short (boys hit the growth spurt later than girls). One study showed that fifty-seven percent of the fellows were dreadfully concerned about blackheads and pimples, and a high percentage of the girls were upset because their nose was too large, or because they were "homely." Later the supposed "defect" often disappears. Natural growth takes care of it. But the memory (in the form of feelings about oneself) often lingers on. And this is a problem. One study showed that of every ten young teen fellows with low strength, six were shy and had later adjustment problems. They had absorbed the idea that they were inadequate, or failures, because of their physique. And that idea became a part of their personalities.

Not all physical characteristics can be outgrown. Some people will have that big nose for life! So what if the characteristic that bothers you isn't past, but present? What if the characteristic isn't just one of appearances? After all, other aspects of our physical selves limit us too.

Remember Ann, the Canadian girl of chapter 1, who wants to be a missionary nurse? Ann is troubled because she failed her freshman year and now is doing poorly in both science and math. Ann, highly motivated, isn't a goof-off. She studies, but she just can't cut it academically. When the brains were passed out, as we used to cruelly say, she must have been behind a tree.

How is Ann going to react to her limitation? She wants to be a missionary nurse. She feels God called her for this ministry, that He's even shown her the part of the world in which to serve. What's she to do? She's facing facts, not just feelings.

There are many young people wanting to be beauties, to be athletes, to be doctors or lawyers, whose physical limitations cut them off from their goals. Their feelings are based on the "here and now"; their sense of failure comes from the solid, not the shadow. Maybe yours does too. Maybe you have solid reasons for unhappiness about yourself. What about you?

But it's important to me!

Actually, even those "solid reasons for unhappiness about yourself" may very well *not* cause unhappiness to someone else. Look at Jack; he valued athletic prowess highly. When his body wouldn't respond the way he wanted, he was mortified. A friend with the same problem—that growth spurt, pushing too fast for good coordination—may not be troubled at all. Why? Because to him sports just aren't that important.

Perhaps in the friend's home value was placed on music, and he's enthusiastic about the instruments he's learning to play. To him musical skill is important, and he's good. What happens? While Jack feels worthless, his musical friend gains self-confidence and satisfaction with himself.

It's the same with Ann. She's deeply concerned about her lack of academic ability because it's important to her. After all, she has to graduate to become a nurse. To another girl with Ann's mental equipment but a different goal in life, low grades may well be unimportant and thus untroubling.

Everything would be fine, then, if each of us simply had goals that fit our abilities and our limitations. Too often we don't. Rosenberg has suggested several reasons. The first goes back to what we said in earlier chapters. Our values are often set by others. Dad values sports, and so we soak up his sense of their importance. Mom and dad both graduated Phi Beta Kappa, so high grades, important to them, become important in our life too. Beauty, a quality stressed in a family noted for beautiful women, becomes important to the one homely daughter. "What's important to me" is thus set early in life, before our real talents can be tried, before any conscious personal choice can be made. Other people's values are built into our lives.

The world in which we live also places premiums on certain traits. Rightly or wrongly, high school and college societies prize athletic ability and good looks. Our society prizes making money and status occupations. Values unconsciously built into our lives by the world we live in can also shape our feelings about ourselves and our worth. When our abilities don't fit in, we're going to feel the strain and be tempted to underrate ourselves.

What to do?

So far in this chapter we've suggested some important ideas. Feelings about ourselves can be formed by our reaction to our physical selves. Such feelings may color our sense of self-worth through life, even after the original cause has been outgrown. Other physical limitations (of looks, size, intelligence, etc.) are not outgrown. We are forced to live with them. But even these limitations aren't a problem, *unless they keep us from something we see as important.* In that case, they can make a person feel a failure.

What can we do to overcome such feelings?

Accept our limitations. This means, first of all, to admit our weaknesses to ourselves. If you're not an all-A student (even though you study hard, and even if the rest of the family is smart), you need to face that fact honestly.

But accepting limitations involves more than just admitting them. Some young people admit they aren't A students—and hate themselves for it. Accepting limitations means putting them in perspective, not letting them pull your picture of yourself askew. It means looking honestly at yourself and saying, "I'm not an A student. And you know what? I still like myself! I'm still worthwhile!"

If you're a Christian, this is especially true for you. A sovereign God has shaped you for a purpose. The Bible says that under Christ's direction "the whole body is fitted together perfectly, and each part in its own special way helps the other parts" (Eph. 4:16). This means just one thing: both your strengths and limitations were planned by God. Your personality was created to fit you for a unique place in His plan. In your own special way you're able to help others, the "other parts" of His body, and so you become eternally valuable to God and to them.

One psychologist points out, "An adolescent needs to prove something to maintain his self-confidence. A mature person (including many chronological adolescents) has usually grown beyond this particular need—he has inward security without esteem-bolstering 'proofs.'" If you can take it on faith that you are worthwhile, you'll not have to constantly prove yourself. Then you'll be free to try new avenues to a richer life. But what about those things that are so desperately important to us?

Examine your values. The fact that "what's important to me" is often determined by others is important to face. Looking back at the illustrations given in this chapter, we can see on the accompanying chart (Fig. 6) how it works.

It's easy to see how those unconscious forces that shape personality (responding to others' expectations, and imitating) have imposed on us values we did not necessarily choose. Oh, they're our values now; they are "important to me." But we are still marching to someone else's tune; we're still living as a child, dependent on someone else's thoughts and ideas.

Figure 6

Problem	Value	Source
big body, but poor coordination	athletic prowess	dad's desires; schoolmates
failure to get A's	high intelligence	parents' premium on grades
low grades	desire to be a missionary nurse	self-chosen goal; sense of God's will
big nose	beauty	family's pride in its beautiful women

What can we do? Choose for ourselves. Sit down and look carefully at what's important to us, and ask, "Is this *really* important? Is this value one which I should stake my life on? Is it really a valid criterion of my worth?"

Remember what it is that separates the man of character from the boy, the adult from the child, the mature from the immature? It is the decision to live by self-chosen values instead of values taken over unthinkingly from others. And this choice should be made by criteria laid down in Scripture—by God's set of standards, not man's.

When you *do* choose, when you get your values in perspective, a change of feelings will follow. And then life will get back in balance. For then feelings will fit the facts, and fit faith.

And that's the way things are with a for-real person.

Steps to take

1. Jot down any physical characteristics—not just looks but other inherited characteristics too—that affect your feelings about yourself.

2. Will some of them be outgrown? Look over the memory-lingers-on section and cross off any problems that are, or will be, outgrown.

3. Construct a chart relating the remaining characteristics to values and their source (see page 59).

4. For insight into God's value system, read: 1 Corinthians 13; 2 Timothy 2:21-26; Titus 2:1-10.

5

In the shadows

An eighteen-year-old Michigan boy asked a good question. "Should parents dominate a teen's life?"

What he meant was clear. How can I be "for real" if I have to live without freedom to be myself? If I have to walk in the shadow cast by my dad's standards, or my mom's convictions, which aren't necessarily mine?

That's the way a lot of youth feel today. An eighteen-year-old Oklahoma City teen said, "The biggest problem I and many of my friends have is, how can you always obey parents when they are so far out of it? I always try to obey, since I have my feet under their table, but it's often difficult. They just don't seem to understand my side of things."

Two fifteen-year-old Michigan girls write in this same vein. "I have a problem at home concerning my parents," says rural Sally. "I would like to know what to do to get better relationships with them. My biggest problem is wanting to do things that they won't permit me to do. I know they have my best interests at heart, but it doesn't seem fair for them to treat me this way."

Sandy, from a small town, feels much the same way. "My parents don't think I can overcome temptations, so I can't date. I know I can overcome them because I've had a chance to decide and I decided against it. Even though I wanted to do this, I made the right decision. So how can I change their minds?"

Sociologist Earnest A. Smith believes that parent-youth conflicts are normal and that "parents should see in such conflicts healthy progress toward independence and maturity."[1] Perhaps so. But most parents don't. The demand for independence and responsibility that flares up in their once-docile child is both puzzling and threatening.

Why puzzling? Because parents don't really know just how a teen-ager should be expected to act. One psychologist points out that "a peculiar problem in our society is the double standard which many parents use in judging their teen-age offspring. In some instances, they are expected to act as young adults and are judged accordingly, while in other cases, they are treated as children."[2]

Little battle, big war

The conflicting desires of young people and the uncertainty of parents (who, after all, are going through this experience for the first time too) lead to many little battles. In fact, it's not unusual for battles to become a way of life during this period.

Take the fourteen-year-old California girl who writes, "I have prayed about it (the problem is getting along with my mother) for some time. I guess the Lord hasn't answered this prayer because of lack of faith. I love my mother, but we have opposite views on everything."

What are some of the things teens and parents come into conflict over?

Figure 7

Percentage of boys who checked each item as seriously disturbing their relationship with their mothers.

1. Won't let me use the car 85.7%
2. Insists that I eat foods I dislike 82.4%
3. Scolds if my grades aren't as high as others' 82.4%
4. Insists that I tell her what I spend money for 80.0%
5. Pesters me about table manners 74.8%
6. Pesters me about personal habits and manners 68.5%
7. Holds my sister or brother up as an example 66.9%
8. Objects to my riding in car at night 65.7%
9. Won't let me follow vocation of my interest 64.5%
10. Complains about neck or fingernails being dirty 55.7%

Figure 8

Percentage of girls who checked each item as seriously disturbing their relationship with their mothers

1. Objects to my going riding at night with boys 87.4%
2. Scolds if my grades aren't as high as others' 85.9%
3. Insists that I eat foods I dislike 83.8%
4. Insists I take my sister or brother with me 82.3%
5. Insists that I tell her what I spend money for 81.2%
6. Spends time out, she is never at home 78.0%
7. Holds my sister or brother up as an example 75.8%
8. Won't let me use the car 70.8%
9. Pesters me about personal habits and manners 70.0%
10. Insists that I go with friends of her choice 69.7%

Figures 7 and 8 show issues that teens said were causing major conflicts with their mothers, or that were so

disturbing in the past that they caused much unhappiness.

Look them over again. Are most of these really big issues? Insists I eat food I don't like. Pesters me about table manners. Won't let me use the car. Scolds about school grades. Big issues? Of course not, not in themselves.

But it's in such skirmishes that the big war, the war for freedom and independence, is usually fought. Underlying it all, too often unrecognized by either combatant, is the need of a young person to be free to live as he or she may choose. In everyone there is a pressure, a need, pushing him to become independent. This desire drags a person on the edge of adulthood into conflict with his parents and with himself. A teen-ager trying to find himself is pushed and pulled by conflicting desires for security and freedom. Parents are uncertain, seeing their emergent youth now as a child, now as a grown-up. The tensions lead to conflicts, to tests of parental authority, to struggles to grasp a bit more freedom in order to be yourself. While the battles range over many issues, the war centers on one: freedom to find yourself, freedom to step out of the shadows and to be for real.

Yet, too often when a teen wins skirmishes and thus achieves "freedom," he discovers that he has lost the war. For there is something peculiar about the kind of freedom that brings reality.

Linda's parents wouldn't let her dance, attend movies or even roller-skate. As a result, she felt like a social outcast. So she especially enjoyed taking part with the kids in a square-dance class at her high school. And she felt no qualms about taking part. After all, it wasn't like the dances her folks forbade.

But another girl had doubts. When she asked her mother's advice, she was told to follow Linda's example.

And so Linda's "downfall" was discovered and reported to her parents.

It was a tough decision for her mom and dad. They were zealous church leaders, and surely their daughter *must* be a model of right behavior! Yet, having enjoyed this pleasure before their conversion, they had no suitable explanation for Linda as to why she shouldn't square dance. Even so, the pleasure Linda thought was so innocent and reasonable was denied. She was to tell her gym teacher that she could no longer take part in the class.

What was Linda to do? She was convinced the pleasure was innocent. And she felt that her parents cared more about using her as a status symbol than in her personally. So Linda declared independence. She claimed the freedom to assert herself. She didn't speak to her teacher. She continued to dance.

Linda was never caught, nor did she believe that her activity was sinful. Yet she experienced a sense of guilt so great that she was miserable during basketball games, seeing her gym teacher on the floor and knowing that she was not being honest with her.

Why hadn't freedom satisfied? Why hadn't Linda's decision to follow her own judgment, to choose her own way, brought with it a sense of adulthood? Because the freedom that brings a sense of fulfillment *is always limited by an individual's sense of right and wrong.* The Bible says it this way: "Live as free men, yet without using your freedom as a pretext for evil" (1 Peter 2:16 RSV). And Linda, committed as a Christian to the belief that "children must always obey . . . fathers and mothers, for that pleases the Lord" (Col. 3:20), had used her freedom as a basis for disobedience.

This is a trap many fall into. They proclaim their independence from parents and, on the basis of personal freedom, choose to act in a way they believe is wrong. Whatever this may bring, it does not bring us closer to being a for-real person.

What are the options?

An Oak Park, Illinois, fellow was in a situation much like Linda's.

> I didn't dance or go to movies, and my parents were against both. After reading the Bible and praying about it, I felt that I could do both if I used discretion in them (i.e., watch where I go). I discussed this with my parents and they went along with it.

This is one option. Exercise your right to decide on your own convictions, but *voluntarily limit your freedom to act by subjecting yourself to your parents.* In this one case, at least, the parents then granted the freedom to act in line with the convictions.

But what if they hadn't? What if they had been shocked,

and, in a great flare of anger, forbade him ever to mention movies or dancing again? How then could he ever reach reality? How can anyone be "for real" if he's not allowed to be himself?

Strangely enough, either example of parental reaction—extending a teen more freedom, or fiercely denying it—provides him with an opportunity to act as a free and independent person. You see, in either case the teen *has* the necessary freedom. He is free to choose.

No one has to be allowed to do as he pleases to be free to make a choice. Even when teens are restricted by parents there is a choice for them to make. One may choose to sulk and suffer. Another may choose to strike back in anger and bitterness. Another may simply agree, and then do the forbidden thing behind his parents' backs. Another may choose to submit because he has to; he "has his feet under their table." But there is another choice. A teen can graciously submit and obey because he believes obedience is right.

This final action—swallowing disappointment and bitterness at unfair treatment (for, in all honesty, parental treatment of teens often *is unfair*), in order to submit to parents *because it's the right thing to do*—is one of the most significant, demanding and "adult" choices a teen under pressure can make. The teen who makes this choice moves a giant step toward becoming a for-real person.

What then does it take for a person living in the shadow of his parents to discover himself, to become a real person in his own right?

Recognize this issue. Don't make the mistake of believing that freedom from parental restrictions is the issue or solution to your problems. We've seen that conflicts arise from complex pressures on both parents and teens. Deep down, what a person desires is not total freedom but a sense of reality, an awareness of his ability to live maturely, by choice.

It's true that many parents are "out of it." Many fail to understand teen problems and pressures, and the whole pattern of a world that has changed fantastically in twenty years. Many parents fall far short of the ideal. But then, most teens aren't ideal either, and sometimes their behavior is thoughtless, inconsistent and demanding.

If we could all focus on the issue, instead of on people, it would be much easier to "be humble and gentle." To "be patient with each other, making allowance for each other's faults because of your love" (Eph. 4:2-3).

When you realize that the issue is maturity, it's much easier to move toward it.

Understand the freedom you seek. An infant demands instant satisfaction for all his desires. If he's hungry, he cries until someone puts a bottle in his mouth. If his bowels are full, he relieves them. His desires are all that matter, and he loudly demands the freedom to do and to have what he wants.

This infant kind of freedom is not the freedom you want. Anyone who sees that maturity is the issue in parental conflicts must face this fact: A mature person is someone who has learned to deny himself the immediate satisfaction of his desires for a higher, self-chosen purpose. He has learned to live by self-chosen values, not by his feelings.

Funny, isn't it? To become a real self, you must deny yourself. But it's true.

For Linda the decision to deny herself the pleasure of square dancing in order to obey her parents would have brought her closer to maturity. The decision to gratify her desires not only brought guilt but forced her back, away from reality.

For a Christian teen, God's standard is firm and clear: "You must always obey your father and mother." That hurts. Even when they're unfair? And the answer comes: "Turn away from evil and do good; try to live in peace even if you must run after it to catch and hold it" (1 Peter 3:11). In the journey toward reality, each of us must deny himself complete independence; each must by faith commit himself to a set of standards that both limits and gives meaning to his freedom.

Strangely, this is the freedom we seek. Not a freedom to "do as we please," but freedom limited by what is right.

You don't have to believe it. But you won't reach reality until you choose it.

Use the freedom you have. Once you choose to be free within a framework of standards, you can step out of the shadows and begin to live life on your own. If your parents grant you the freedom to choose your hours, your friends, your amusements—use it! Test your desires against the standards you freely choose, and do what you believe is right. You'll discover by yourself what you really want.

If your parents insist on deciding for you in areas where you've developed your own convictions and ideas, you can still use your freedom. Even though it hurts to feel their lack of trust, you can freely choose what you know is right, and give in.

One eighteen-year-old Michigan girl says, "It works! I found that if you have the right attitude and overcome your natural rebelliousness and simply do what they say, you will get along much better." But even more important than the better relationships at home, you'll be acting "on your own," freely choosing in an adult way to limit yourself by what you believe is right. And in this self-chosen subjection you yourself will find what you really want.

Sometimes this is hard for a young person to grasp. An adult, a person who "makes his own decisions," really isn't any more free than a teen-ager. He too must live in subjection. Dad can't take off from work to go fishing— not if he's going to support the family. When my wife and I were first married we enjoyed going out to eat, attending the Gilbert and Sullivan operettas staged at the University of Michigan, and participating in many other affairs. But when we had a child we gave up many of the things we had enjoyed. We were not free to do as we pleased. We were free only to decide within the limits of our circumstances. But we were free to choose what we believed was right.

The Apostle Paul often spoke of his authority over the churches and over other believers. Yet he too placed limits on himself. Once some new Christians in Corinth became upset because others bought meat at temple meat markets, and that meat had been offered to idols. Paul was convinced that since "an idol has no real existence" (1 Cor. 8:4 RSV), he was free to eat. Yet he wrote, "If food is a cause of my brother's falling, I will never eat meat, lest I cause my brother to fall" (1 Cor. 8:13 RSV). He chose to limit his freedom by a higher law, that of love for others.

It's not easy, this finding yourself by choosing limits on your own freedom, this earning your own self-respect. But that's what it takes. That's being for real.

Steps to take

1. Jot down "trouble spots" in your relationship with your parents. Where do you feel your ideas and convictions are overshadowed by theirs?

2. Study the last section of the chapter. Beside each trouble spot you listed, write any convictions or

beliefs you hold which limit your freedom in them.

3. Finally, decide what freedom you do have, and how you will use it. Then use it.

6

Out to be "in"?

Carol, a Connecticut girl, faced the pressure of popularity soon after she entered high school.

When I was a young teen-ager in high school, I wanted very much to be in the "in" crowd. I felt that the most popular kids were the cheerleaders and I thought I'd make my breakthrough by becoming a cheerleader. I just needed a sense of security and of being wanted by my classmates.

But then it started bothering me. As a Christian, did I have a right to want to be in the "in" crowd? Would I "fall away" if I became a cheerleader? These questions really bothered me and I didn't have the answers. So I decided to talk to some adults who might be able to help.

I asked my parents and they, of course, seemed to be no help. Parents never seem helpful at that age. Dad was worried that his "poor little girl" would be corrupted by the world. Mom felt that being a cheerleader would be great, yet she had reservations. Sure, she wanted me to have friends, but would I have to compromise?

I then asked a youth leader at our church, something I never should have done. And I got the usual reply: "Pray about it." Thanks. I had been doing that. What I needed was help!

So I turned to my teen-aged friends and together we investigated the reputation of the cheerleaders. We found out exactly what connotations cheerleading carried with it and if it would be possible for one person to change this idea.

The problem was really a difficult one but it all boiled down to: Does a Christian have the right to be respected, approved, and "in" with the peer group? None of the adults seemed able to help and from what Mom says now, they were really frustrated about what to do. They wanted me to have friends, but really didn't trust my convictions.

Carol ran head on into some of the hard facts about life in the teen-age world.

A lonely battlefield

Carol was frustrated when her folks couldn't help her or even understand the issue she faced. Sometimes teens are frustrated because parents try!

One day a mother in our church asked me to talk to her teen-age daughter. She couldn't understand what had happened to make her sweet, cooperative child so opinionated and disagreeable. Especially about clothes. Why, the girl even wanted satin pants. She'd look like a hood!

Later I did talk with the daughter. The conflict with her mother troubled her too, especially in regard to clothes. Why, everyone in her crowd at school wore satin pants and her mother was calling them "hoody"! *She* knew what hoods wore, and she wouldn't be caught dead in their clothing.

She knew, mom didn't. That's an important thing to recognize about the world you now live in. Outsiders really don't understand it. They're not supposed to. The talk, the clothes, the music, the fads, the things to do for kicks, are special for insiders. They're not for those on the outside. It's through things like these that teens can create a separate world for themselves, a world that exists alongside the adult world but is distinct from it.

Why a separate world for youth? Probably because there's no place for teens in the world of adults. No place, that is, where teens can be accepted, can feel they belong, can be given and accept responsibility, can be free to be themselves. Adults can't even decide when a young person is old enough to be considered "one of us." When is a teen "adult" enough to drive? When is he adult enough to vote? Eighteen. To join the military? To be married? To own property? To be employed? To serve on a board at church?

No, teens don't have a place in the adult world. Not as equals. Not as persons in their own right. And so, rejected by adult society and cemented together by each one's growing need for independence from parents, youth in high school and college create their own society, their own world, to which adults are strangers.

Wanting to be "in"

This was disturbing to Carol. She found that she wanted very much to be "in." She doubted whether it was *right* to "want to be respected, approved, and 'in' with the peer group." But there was no doubt about her desire.

Actually, wanting to be "in" is *not* wrong. The need to be accepted, to be a part, to belong, is basic. We all share it. For a person just striking out on his own and cutting one by one the cords of dependency at home, to *belong* in his own new world is dreadfully important.

Yet some Christian teens seem troubled by these desires. Some tend to withdraw from their world as the real issue becomes clouded with fears of compromise. Should a Christian be really involved in the school and its activities? "I couldn't decide," writes a girl from Illinois. "Was that 'being yoked together' with unbelievers?"

Others feel rather bitter that so many Christian teens fail to fit into the teen-age world. An eighteen-year-old Vermonter, now in college, says, "The Christian teen-ager tends to be an isolationist: he lacks the maturity and courage to face the world." A California girl adds, "Christians sticking just to

THE "IN" SWIM

themselves give others the feeling they're cliquish and that they are Christians because they don't have the ability or interest to get in other activities, or because they don't care about others."

Certainly as Christians we have to be in the world, even though distinctively not of it.

Why does a young person need to belong? Many sociologists and researchers have pointed out reasons. Here are some:

Belonging helps gain independence. The Illinois girl who wondered if joining school clubs was being "unequally yoked" discovered this. She later "talked to friends who knew what I stood for. I joined the clubs and met tons of kids with whom I had personal contact and a chance to share Christ." When you learn to live successfully in a world not dominated by your parents, you gain self-confidence. You discover that you *can* solve your own problems. A person on the edge of reality needs this kind of experience.

Belonging gives opportunities to share and to grow as a person. Take a look at the experience of Betsy, a fifteen-year-old Arizonan. Betsy had problems because she didn't want to compromise her standards. "I never could get used to people coming up and asking me why I never went to dances, etc. Sometimes I was frightened people would ask me questions I couldn't answer." But Betsy belonged in a group of other Christian kids. "The kids at church got together and we all prayed for our lives in school, at work, on dates, etc. God gave me more strength than I ever expected and He led me to know people that I was even frightened of."

To Betsy the opportunity to share her needs and problems with others in her world became a vital source of strength, and a channel through which God answered prayer. Through this shared experience with others she was able to grow to the point where she overcame her fear of others, and found freedom to enjoy them. This too is part of being for real.

Belonging helps establish a sense of identity. No one wants to go through life pointed out as "Him? Oh, that's the son of Jack Lambe, the lawyer." Being for real isn't being "the son of" anybody. It's being yourself. In the teen-age world you have a chance to *be* you, to be evaluated and accepted for your own personal qualities and attributes. This is important too, and also helps a person find himself.

There are other reasons. *Belonging helps you learn how to get along with others. Belonging helps you get to know others of the opposite sex. Belonging gives you a chance to learn to evaluate people.* And so on. All these values can be summed up as one important fact: *you can't become for real alone.* To grow as a person, to learn to live on your own, you must "find yourself" in relationship to others.

So really it's a good thing, this desire to be "in." Just when you *need* to belong in your world of young people, you want to belong. Carol, and others like her, need not draw back in guilty fear when they feel the desire. It's natural to want to belong. And it's necessary.

On what terms?

Carol was quick to spot a pathway to the popularity and status she wanted in her world. Cheerleading. But then, she wrote, "It started bothering me." Why? She began to worry about the price she might have to pay for acceptance.

Carol took the right approach in evaluating her problem. She looked at the terms before she bought the product. "I turned to my teen-age friends and together we investigated the reputation of the cheerleaders. We found out exactly what connotations cheerleading carried with it. . . ."

There are special rules by which youth play the game of life. Some of them are general, for the whole community. Most of these are morally neutral. Clothing fads, for instance, usually are. The satin pants, mom to the contrary, were all right. Even hairstyles (as hard as this may be for adults to recognize) need not have any moral or immoral overtones. And the language—that particular way of saying things that shifts from year to year—is an important mark of membership in the teen world. These may grate on adults. But they are part of fitting in.

But the belonging that we all long for demands more. It requires a close association with a special group of friends. In these special groups (cliques, gangs, crowds) there exist other rules, other more distinctive patterns of behavior. Jack got in with a crowd that smoked and swore and drank.

> My high school was large (3,000 students), and there were many cliques. There was the popular athletic, cheerleading and school leader set, the intellectual group, the dramatic and musical set, different groups due to one particular interest. And there was a group of the more grossly "unnice" kids—the rebels, lawbreakers, who enjoyed the reputation of being tough and able to do anything or drink anything. Unfortunately this latter group was the easiest in which to be accepted, so many new kids, with the desire to belong and be accepted by a group of friends, often ended up with a bad crowd.

Too often, propelled by a desire to "be wanted by my classmates," a teen will join the first group that accepts him. Nearly always this is the "wrong" crowd.

However, for a Christian the solution isn't outright rejection of such frendships. The Apostle Paul once corrected some people who thought withdrawal was the answer.

"When I wrote to you before I said not to mix with evil people. But when I said that, I wasn't talking about unbelievers who live in sexual sin, or are greedy cheats and thieves and idol worshipers. For you can't live in this world without being with people like that" (1 Cor. 5:9-10).

Don't misunderstand at this point. It is important to develop friendships with those who think and believe as you do. *They* should be your close friends. Every person, no matter how mature, needs support and the fellowship of others committed to the same standards and values.

Sometimes making such friends isn't easy. Too often Christian teens form cliques that block others out. Often outsiders sense the rejection of such closed fellowships. And it really hurts.

No one actually branded us with the title, but Gladys, Vicky and I were the spiritual in-group of the church. Since we lived a few blocks from each other, we'd walk to church together, walk to school together and plan to attend special meetings together.

What really blew the situation was the arrival in church of several new young people. We tried to show some friendliness by talking to them and inviting them to our youth group, but there was never a real sense of inclusion in the group. There was almost the feeling of resentment in the air when a "new person" tried to include himself in our trio. Some of these young people left the church. We couldn't determine why at the time.

If you're on the outside looking in, the advice, "Choose your special group of friends carefully," may seem a cruel joke. It's not. The time and the hurt it may take to find your place will be worth it.

There are several requirements, then, for fitting in:

1. You need to fit into the general patterns of youth life. That's not hard. It comes naturally.

2. You need a closer association with a few special friends. It's important that this group be carefully chosen to match your beliefs and standards. This is important for any Christian. Paul stresses this kind of association when he writes to adults, "Let there be no sex sin, impurity or greed among you. Let no one be able to accuse you of any such things. Dirty stories, foul talk and coarse jokes—these are not for you. Instead, remind each other of God's goodness and be thankful" (Eph. 5:3-4).

Don't worry that if you become a member of such a holy group you'll have no chance to test your standards. Rub daily against others too. The chances will come, hard and fast!

3. You need a passport other than conformity. And that passport is respect, earned by being a for-real person, choosing your own values and living steadfastly according to them.

That's what it takes to fit in. But what does it take to be for real?

Got what it takes?

"I could resist these temptations," says Jack, "But why don't I?" The temptations in themselves have little hold. But deep down Jack feels that he hasn't got what it takes to buck his friends. Each time he denies himself and his beliefs in order to conform, this uncertainty about himself grows.

What can help you to make that right decision the next time *you're* sweating under pressure from your peers?

You need to understand your feelings. It's all right to want to belong. We've even seen that belonging is important, an aid in the struggle to be "for real." Yet, many teens misread their desire in two respects. Why is it there, and what will satisfy it?

Too often belonging is viewed as an end in itself. When this happens, belonging is twisted into "popularity." "Popularity was my supreme goal," writes a Missouri girl. She was in trouble.

Life is too big and too important to have a year or two at the top of some high school society as its goal. God didn't implant the urge to be accepted so we could make popularity an idol.

But He did have a purpose. We looked at it earlier. Some day every young person will have to find a place in adult society. Hopefully, an important place. Yet, to fit into this life he will have to be emotionally independent of his parents. He will need to know how to relate effectively to others. He will need confidence, that assurance that he has what it takes to be himself. It's for these reasons that it's important to belong, for in belonging, all these benefits can be won.

Sadly, most of those who sacrifice themselves for popularity don't attain their goals. And they discover too that popularity does not satisfy. Many studies have shown that the top kids, the leaders, the "in" fellows and girls, feel less secure and accepted than teens who have one or two close friends with whom they can share. That's the second thing. What will satisfy the need for belonging? Popularity? No. It takes real friends, growing, sharing, and being yourself.

Years ago the apostle Paul outlined a choice similar to the one many teens must make as he described some men who vied for popularity in the churches. "Their trouble is that they are only comparing themselves with each other, and measuring themselves against their own little ideas. But," he went on, "we will not boast of authority we do not have. Our goal is to measure up to God's plan for us" (2 Cor. 10:12-13). That's a pretty clear choice.

You *can* choose fleeting popularity as your goal. But it won't give you what you want—or need.

Evaluate your world. Don't make the mistake of thinking that only in the teen-age world will you feel pressures to conform. There are worlds inside the adult world too. The businessman lives in the "business world," the lawyer in the "professional world," the factory worker in the "labor world." Each of these worlds has its own values, standards and patterns of life. And each exerts strong pressures to make its members conform.

Remember chapter 3? The tension between living by someone else's standards or by our own self-chosen ones is always with us. And it's on that issue that being for real hinges.

In your personal struggles to find and be yourself, you *have* to evaluate your world. You can't exchange one form of unreality (being a carbon copy of parents) for another (being a carbon copy of your friends). You have to learn to live on your own, "to see clearly the difference between right and wrong, and to be inwardly clean" (Phil. 1:10).

That's why Carol's course of action was so right. She wanted to be in, but she stopped to study the connotations of becoming a cheerleader. When you stop to study the patterns of life in your world, and measure them against the standards you hold, you're headed for reality.

So don't duck your challenges. Don't cut yourself off from kids whose standards are different from yours. But "don't live to make a good impression on others" either (Phil. 2:3). Instead, determine to live in the world of other teens by your choice—not theirs.

You don't have to be forced into the mold of your world in order to belong. And you *can't* live forced into its mold. Not if you want to find yourself. Not if you want to be real.

Steps to take

1. Suppose Jack (p. 81) bucks his friends and stands up for his convictions, only to find himself "out" of the gang? If you were in Jack's position, how would you feel? What would you do next?

2. Suppose Carol discovers the cheerleaders do have bad reputations but that the activities connected with cheerleading have no bad connections? If you were in Carol's situation, what would you do? Why?

3. Are there any areas in which you feel a conflict between your standards and pressures from your world? Jot them down. Go back over the chapter and analyze your handling of each conflict you jotted down. Do you withdraw? Or conform? Or be for real? Outline the issues in each case as carefully as you can, by yourself or in discussion with friends. Then decide.

7

Free to choose

When Carol finished investigating the cheerleaders, she was still confused. Their reputation in her high school was not good. Yet, there didn't seem to be any bad connotations about their responsibilities. Discussion of the pros and cons with her friends didn't take her far. Even praying about it and studying the Bible provided no clear-cut solution.

Finally, in complete uncertainty, "I decided that I would approach the 'open door' of opportunity and if the Lord didn't want me to try, He'd close it. That He did. I was sick the whole week of tryouts."

But it's not often that God spells out our decisions for us!

This, of course, is one source of "the misery of adolescence," as Ralph put it. Freedom isn't easy, for freedom means having to decide. And usually the choices aren't marked with road signs, one saying, "This way is God's will," and all the others, "Detour."

At the beginning of this book I suggested that some-

thing special characterizes a for-real person: he is what he seems to be.

In later chapters we saw that being for real as a person does not, however, mean simply giving rein to our impulses. That's being for real for a baby! All he is is impulses. So when he lets loose, he is being what he seems to be.

But you and I aren't babies. We're more than impulses. Over the years our impulses have been controlled and channeled by the expectations of others. In the process we've developed ideas of right and wrong. By now these are as much a part of us as the impulses. So being for real can't mean acting like a baby and following every impulse. It must mean being the kind of persons we are, persons with standards by which to guide, control and judge our impulses and desires.

Then too I suggested that there is something special about the standards of a for-real person. They are self-chosen. "Self-chosen" doesn't mean that we make them up ourselves, any more than we accept, without thought or evaluation, the standards of others. It does mean that we _freely and consciously choose to apply and live by standards._

None of this seems especially difficult to understand. But when a person—even a Christian, who believes that God has given clear-cut, authoritative standards—tries to live this way, he finds that the for-real life is both difficult and challenging.

A test case

Glance again at Carol. If you thought through the second Steps-to-take question in the last chapter, you recognized some of her difficulties. Carol found both pros and cons in her balances. How could she tell which course was right?

What have other teens experienced in their relationships with non-Christians? If you listen to a young Michigan girl, now in college, Carol's course seems clear.

> I especially dated one non-Christian fella at the end of my senior year, and we had some very wonderful talks, experiences, and sharing times together. He was interested in my Christian ideas, and I learned much from listening to and knowing him. We even fell in love—or at least loved each other dearly. He is now engaged to another girl. (I had prayed the Lord would bless our relationship and break it up, romantically, when it got too close.) He's not yet a Christian, but I think he will be someday. Maybe my dating him gave me the chance to plant the seed.

For the other side, listen to this Virginia girl:

> Though my parents were Christian, they were quite naive to the situations of public high school. I was led into sin gradually by a handsome blond. The aftereffects were terrible—guilt, fear, etc. They still affect me, though it is very much in the past.

Better listen to her experience before you rush out to date an unsaved fellow for the chance to witness! Of course, on the other hand, the Michigan girl did witness, and—

Even keeping off the emotionally charged "dating" level, others have no clear-cut answers for someone like Carol.

In chapter 3 we heard from a Delaware teen who, in his junior year of high school, realized he hadn't been involved with his unsaved classmates. After prayer he promised the Lord he would make friends, for His sake. "As a result," he reported, "two people have come to a saving knowledge, and I feel at ease to talk about my Savior." Pretty convincing? Carol definitely ought to get involved?

Well, here's the other side. "I have trouble with my relationship with non-Christians. It's so easy to go along with the crowd and it's so hard to witness." And from a nineteen-year-old girl who wrote me on this subject:

> I had almost no Christian close friends, mainly because there were hardly any young people my age in our church. And I was struggling with compromise, and felt very lonely. Emphasize, *please,* the danger of getting dragged down in trying to "reach" others.

So far we've just listened to people. Why not go to the source book? Let's look to Scripture. What might Carol find in the Word to suggest a possible course of action?

Let's try to think along with her.

Hm. The Bible! That's where I'll find a clear answer. What's this now? "If someone who isn't a Christian asks you out to dinner, go ahead, accept the invitation if you want to" (1 Cor. 10:27). _Well, that seems to free me to associate. But then, what's this here in Ephesians? Oh, yes._ "Dirty stories, foul talk and coarse jokes—these are not for you" (Eph. 5:4). _Wouldn't I have to associate with folks like that? Probably. It doesn't seem right to get identified with such a crowd._

Wait a minute. What's this? "When I wrote you . . . not to mix with evil people. . . . I wasn't talking about unbelievers" (1 Cor. 5:9-10). _Well. It's all right then. Guess I'd better rush out and sign up for tryouts._

Oops. What's this now? "Be careful. If you are thinking, 'Oh, I would never behave like that'—let this be a warning to you. For you too may fall into sin" (1 Cor. 10:12). _Well. Guess maybe I'd better not! No use running that kind of risk._

Of course, the Bible does say, "What's the use of saying that you have faith and are a Christian if you aren't proving it by helping others?" (James 2:14). _Can I really justify not getting involved just because of fear? No, I have to take the chance. I'll do it!_

Then again, it says here, "You must be even more careful to do the good things that result from being saved, obeying God with deep reverence, shrinking back from all that might displease him" (Phil. 2:12). _Well, it certainly might displease God. Of course, maybe Paul took the same chance. He did say,_ "Whatever a person is like, I try to find common ground with him so that he will let me tell him about Christ" (1 Cor. 9:22). _And cheerleading is common ground. So—_

What was Carol to do? Look as she would, Carol just couldn't find a clear-cut rule that would bail her out of her confusion. And in many cases, you won't either! That's the difficulty.

Standards are not rules

Often we make the mistake of viewing biblical standards simply as rules or laws. They aren't.

Does this mean that the Word of God is not objectively true, an eternal expression of the character and will of God? Of course not! It is. It simply means that in the complications of life it is often difficult to see *which* principles are to govern a particular situation.

Take the case of building friendships with non-Christians. It may be right for one person to build a friendship, and wrong for another *in the same situation!* The first may be stronger in his Christian experience and be able to stand the pressures; the second may be younger and not ready for this challenge. Or the first may approach friendship for the right motive, the second from a wrong motive. Again, it may be wrong for the one person to attempt to establish a relationship with a particular individual or group at one time, and yet the right thing at another. Why? For many possible reasons—his own strength, or motive, or because God has not yet prepared his friends, etc.

None of this indicates that we are free from standards, or that the biblical standards are inconsistent. Some things are never right. Premarital sex, for instance, is unquestionably in this category. But we face other choices that are not "unquestionably" right or wrong. And then we have to evaluate the situation, examine our standards, and look in complete dependence to God to guide us to the right choice.

It's only when we view standards like this, as guiding principles which we are individually responsible to apply, that we have an opportunity to be for real. Life by rules, by code, by inflexible laws expressed as dos and don'ts, stifles maturity. We have to take responsibility.

Difficult? Yes! For there's always the possibility of a mistake. And somehow this new responsibility may bring a time of seeming misery to a person on the edge of reality. Why? For several reasons.

Being used to a rule-type life. The child lives by rules that parents set, rules that are usually clear-cut. Don't go to movies. Don't stay out after ten. Do your homework before you watch television. Finish the food on your plate. Life on this level is patterned and relatively easy. We have little to decide—just whether to obey or not.

Shifting over to live by standards that you choose and that you have to apply yourself isn't easy!

Not knowing your own standards well enough. Many a Christian teen announces that he's leaving church and the study of the Bible because he has "heard all that stuff." It may be that poor materials and poor teaching are not meeting needs. But a teen, often brought up with a rule-type view of God's Word, is only now ready to *begin* to learn! To a person living by choice the Bible is no luxury; it's a necessity. Without deep personal involvement in Scripture, standards are inevitably influenced and shaped by others.

Not being fully aware of the role of motive. Under rule-type life, external conformity is the issue that is judged. Both the person himself and others measure him by the way he fits the pattern they have established.

Reality is different. Motive, not conformity, becomes the norm. Have you ever read 1 Corinthians 13? Read it. It catalogs all the things men *do* to please God, and pronounces, in regard to each thing, that if I "have not love, I am nothing."

It's hard to shift over from considering only externals and forms and rules to consider heart attitude. But that's what it takes to live in reality.

Being for real, then, doesn't come easily. It's not like the need to shave—automatically yours with age! You have to take matters in your own hands. You have to act. Most of all, perhaps, you have to have courage to be for real.

A discouraging prospect?

Does this seem discouraging?

It often looks that way. Particularly if you've tried and failed. Often, after repeated failures, we feel there's no hope. Reality may be discovered by others, but in *my* circumstances, with *my* background, with the way my life has been warped by my parents, with the bad reputation I have, with the poor testimony I've been, there's just no use trying.

Possibly if we were talking right now, I might excuse you on the basis of things like these. Or you yourself might excuse others. But *you can never excuse yourself.*

Why? Because, no matter what your past, when you find yourself in a conflict situation, *you know that you have the freedom to choose.* You may make a choice you hate. The Apostle Paul did at times (see Rom. 7:15). But you know that *you* chose.

Awareness of this responsibility is both a burden and a cause of hope. It becomes a burden if we constantly live out our mistakes. If we constantly think of things we *could* have said, but didn't. If we curse ourselves for our weaknesses and our past sins. This isn't necessary for the Christian. The Bible says that simple confession to God clears you and restores you to harmony with God and with yourself (1 John 1:9).

But awareness of responsibility is also a source of hope.

You see, if my present were really "determined" by my past, I could have no hope. If I live today, completely controlled or caught in circumstances, I would be helpless. But I'm aware that I can choose! I'm free.

A sixteen-year-old girl's experience illustrates what I mean:

> I started going to a fundamental church but the young people didn't talk to me or include me. They were all concerned about themselves. I went to camp and dedicated my life to the Lord, came back, and started living as God wanted me to. I now tried to treat others as He would. Soon I was president of our youth group.

Did she have reason to blame the others? Certainly! They were clearly at fault. But was there a way out? Yes. One within herself. "I . . . started living as God wanted *me* to."

This is true for all of us who want to live as for-real persons. The place to start is inside. We can learn to use the freedom that we know we have. And we can choose to live by the standards we hold. We have the opportunity to be real.

Steps to take

Write out your answers. Then check yourself by reviewing the chapter.

1. Biblical standards do not give a person the opportunity to be for real. They force him into a mold.
Is this idea true or false? Why?

2. It's often hard for a young person to start living by self-chosen standards. Why?

3. What does knowing that you are free to choose mean to you? Is the idea depressing? Frightening?

8

That no-good-sinner bit

Have you stopped yet to wonder why the author of a *Christian* book to teens starts off by saying "Be for real; let what you seem to be match up with what you are"?

You should wonder. After all, isn't the Christian picture of man rather black? If I live what I *am*, won't sins come to the surface? Wouldn't a for-real Christian almost have to be what he *isn't*?

Take, for instance, the experience of Carl, an eighteen-year-old from Michigan.

I used to think that I was a pretty good Christian. I went to church, had devotions, prayed, and did everything I could to win others to Christ. But it took an operation with a long time to think to make me realize that I wasn't all I thought I was. I started thinking about other things which were important to me: sports, reading, dates, having a good time, and friends. Then it came to me, for professing Christ as my Savior, I had a lot of worldly desires going for me. I discovered many faults and fallacies were really at the center of my life.

Connie, an Arizona teen, was very different from Carl. She was an evangelical "rebel."

> I was unable to communicate with my parents, fought with my siblings, and "followed the crowd." I excused my actions on the hypocrisy I found both at home and at church. My favorite phrase was "I'm my own boss," which unfortunately applied to both spiritual and secular matters. Then, by divine design, I was given a foreign exchange sister, which forced me to develop both a civic and religious responsibility. It was only when I realized I had failed as her example that I was able to acknowledge my own spiritual shallowness, and see that my greatest problem was a basic egocentricity. I, as so many others have, said, "There must be more to life than this."

Carl and Connie, so different on the surface, discovered they were the same down underneath. Carl, the "ideal Christian teen" who witnessed and even had devotions (only seven percent of evangelical teens do!), didn't like what he found when he examined his heart. Connie, the rebel who excused herself by blaming others, labled what she found inside "shallow" and "egocentric."

Strangely, the foundation for becoming a for-real Christian is to recognize this shallowness and egocentricity for what it is.

The under-surface self

Modern psychiatry and Scripture are essentially in harmony when it comes to a view of the under-surface self that Carl and Connie glimpsed. According to Professor Graham T. Blaine, chief of psychiatry at Harvard University,

> Freud's concept of the unconscious, described by him as "a chaos of seething excitement which knows no values, no good and evil, no morality," does not differ very much from the "sinful desires of the flesh" mentioned in a Prot-

estant baptismal service. The irrational force of the Id which compels one to behave in a manner contrary to one's better judgment is also well described in the Bible by St. Paul when he says, "If I do what I would not, it is no more I that do it but sin that dwelleth in me; for I delight in the law of God after the inward man, but I see another law in my members warring against the law of my mind."

In oversimplified language the nature of man, whether viewed in religious or psychiatric terms, makes it difficult for him to control himself or behave in a way that appears rational and reasonable from his own as well as society's point of view. He needs help. . . .[1]

Christian psychiatrist Paul Tournier agrees, and points out that even his colleagues

. . . who describe themselves as unbelievers know well that all men are weak and wretched; that they construct fine edifices of reason, but when it comes to the point they are carried away by their passions; that they all have their noble ideals, but are powerless to conform to them; that they seek to appear strong, but have all sorts of hidden fears in their hearts; that they all have a need to believe in something greater than themselves, and that if they do not follow the true God they fall into childish superstition.[2]

Connie had followed one course. She let the "irrational forces" carry her along and control her actions. She justified her actions as "freedom," and excused herself as more honest than hypocritical believers around her. When she finally saw her impulses in a scriptural light, her excuses were stripped away.

What are these impulses or irrational forces? The Bible portrays them in a number of ways. They're called "the pull of man's own evil thoughts and wishes" (James 1:14); "a whole army of evil desires within you" (James 4:1). Because of them we're pictured as "misled by others and slaves to many evil pleasures and wicked desires," with

INSIDE·O·MOMETER

lives "full of resentment and envy" (Titus 3:3). The things Connie found herself doing were only natural—"expressing the evil within us" because "we started out bad, being born with evil natures, and were under God's anger just like everyone else" (Eph. 2:3).

This is the meaning of that no-good-sinner bit you've heard in church. Not that we can never do a kind or generous thing, but that deep down in the center of our nature is a tragic flaw. It warps our minds to think evil thoughts. It warps our hearts to wrong desires. It warps our will to choose. We can, like Connie, attempt to excuse or justify our actions. But experience brings us all to the point where we realize that the ultimate cause of wrong is within, and beyond our control.

This often is puzzling to the young Christian. Conversion doesn't straighten out the warp. We all still have the irrational forces and impulses a non-Christian has. And we can follow them, as Connie did. Watch out for the result though. For "when you follow your own wrong inclinations your lives will produce these evil results: impure thoughts, eagerness for lustful pleasure, . . . hatred and fighting, jealousy and anger, constant effort to get the best for yourself, complaints and criticisms, the feeling that everyone else is wrong except those in your own little group" (Gal. 5:19-20).

We are told to deaden these evil desires, and to have nothing to do with their outworkings (Col. 3:5). But we are never promised freedom from them. They're there, inside us. And they're going to stay there, whether they show up openly or not.

No dos-and-don'ts life

"Most kids," says a Missouri girl, "have been told since grammar school up the dos and don'ts of Christianity, and the only answer for not doing something is that it is 'bad,' 'not Christian,' etc. Many teens are confronted with non-church-raised kids who think they're way out because they have no reason why they don't do things."

Paul himself was unhappy when some tried to make Christianity a dos-and-don'ts way of life in his day. He wrote:

Since you died . . . with Christ and this has set you free

from following the world's ideas of how to be saved—by doing good and obeying the various rules—why do you keep right on following them anyway, still bound by such rules as not eating, tasting, or even touching certain foods? Such rules are mere human teachings, for food was made to be eaten and used up. These rules may seem good, for rules of this kind require strong devotion and are humiliating and hard on the body, but they have no effect when it comes to conquering a person's evil thoughts and desires. They only make him proud (Col. 2:20-23).

Rules are like this. They seem good. They require strong devotion and self-control. But they have no effect when it comes to conquering what's inside.

When teens get hung up on parental rules insisting— sometimes bitterly—that "this isn't the religion Christ taught," they've missed the point. *Any* ideas can be twisted into rules—including New Testament teachings! Positive biblical standards, such as showing love, speaking to others about Christ, refraining from gossip or other sins, can be misread as rules to live by. And when they are followed as rules, the result is *never* "the religion Christ taught."

Following human rules won't save you. But neither will following the Ten Commandments! The Bible says that "no human being will be justified in his sight [saved] by works of the law, since through the law comes knowledge of sin" (Rom. 3:20 RSV). Even God's standards don't change us. They merely show up the character of the impulses inside. It's by having standards, and seeing how we twist and struggle to avoid them, that the evil character of our inner impulses is known.

God's standards, unlike human rules, not only *may* be good, they are good. Paul calls them "holy and just and good" (Rom. 7:12 RSV). To live up to them also may seem like a challenge requiring "strong devotion" and being "humiliating and hard on the body." The trouble is, as Carl found out, *even living by God's standards has "no effect when it comes to conquering a person's evil thoughts and desires!"*

Carl thought he was a pretty good Christian because he lived up to strong, positive biblical rules. But when he looked inside he saw twisted motives. He had no call for pride, only for confession.

You can complain about your human rules all you want. Call them deadening and unreal. But if you follow only God's standard's as your code, you'll be no better off.

Because *no* code can bring us to reality in our Christian life that God offers freedom from sin *apart* from standards which are viewed as rules. For sin, Paul says, will no longer "Have dominion over you: *for ye are not under the law, but under grace*" (Rom. 6:14 KJV).

No change inside

This is why many a for-real person falls short of being a for-real Christian. Christian or non-Christian can live by self-chosen standards (even standards not sourced in Scripture) and become admirable people. On a human level, such a life can bring a personality into balance and harmony, at least temporarily. But it never produces a for-real Christian.

Since a for-real Christianity is concerned with what's inside rather than with appearances, it's clear that it can't be attained through standards at all! Not even by God's standards, as holy and good as they are. In order to achieve freedom from what's inside and to obtain that for-real Christian experience we want, we have to turn from law to grace.

This is the point of that no-good-sinner bit. Christianity isn't summed up in standards that we're unable to keep. The Christian life isn't just matching up belief and behavior. Christ offers us far more, a dimension of life unimagined by anyone outside, no matter how real he may be as a person.

Both Connie and Carl found this out. "I've found there *is* more to life," she testifies, "not merely existing, but really living each day abundantly." And Carl too tells of a fresh newness to life. "Now I delight in the things I used to do. Now I do them because I enjoy them, not because it's what I'm supposed to do. Now I can surely say that my life is centered in Christ; my life is Christ."

Self-discovery was their first step toward for-real Christianity. It must be your first step too.

Steps to take

1. Who are you most like: Connie or Carl? From memory jot down a brief description of each. Check it, listing any points in which you are like either.

2. If you feel you're more like Connie, look over Galatians 5. Do these things show up in your life? How? What does this tell you about yourself?

3. If you feel you're more like Carl, go over the list you made of ways you're like him. What happens when you analyze the motives for your behavior?

4. If you aren't satisfied with your life as a Christian, write out just what will satisfy you.

9

The mark of reality

An eighteen-year-old Massachusetts girl, now in a Christian college, asks, "What is Christianity? Isn't it just the decision of a person to believe one way? If believing is seeing, why not believe the ways of Mormons or Buddhists, and then 'see' their doctrines?"

It's a question often asked today. Isn't any faith just psychological? Isn't there something in commitment to any set of beliefs that brings life into harmony?

We can readily admit that commitment to a faith—to any faith—as a way of life is helpful. It does have psychological benefits. And, as we've seen earlier in this book, commitment to self-chosen standards can bring a person into a certain harmony with himself. It can make him a for-real person. He can conquer many forms of outbreak of the evil impulses that compose his inner nature, and he can live a good life.

Many faiths give such moral direction. If Christianity promises little more than a divine set of standards to replace those which men have developed for themselves, why choose between them! But when we meet kids like Connie and Carl, we find they don't talk about how they live up to their standards. They talk about something new inside.

We find the same thing in the Bible. The emphasis isn't on codes. It too is concerned about what's inside. What counts with God is that under-surface self that intrudes into even our best acts. And only Christ offers us a change *inside*.

The Bible explains this change inside that we've come to expect in a for-real Christian. Peter writes,

> Now you can have real love for everyone because your souls have been cleansed from selfishness and hatred when you trusted Christ to save you. . . . For you have a new life. It was not passed on to you from your parents . . . it comes from Christ, God's ever-living message to men (1 Peter 1:22-23).

"The person who has been born into God's family does not make a practice of sinning because now God's life is in him," adds the Apostle John (1 John 3:9). That's why the phrase "born again" has become so well worn in evangelical churches. We literally *are* born again, for when we trust Christ as Savior, God sovereignly plants His life in us. This new life, just as real as the old, brings us a completely different set of impulses and desires. These move in harmony with God because they come from Him. Although our natural capacity to love is warped to desire wrong, this new life gives us a capacity to desire what's right. Although our natural capacity to think is warped toward evil thoughts, the new life gives us a capacity to understand and perceive God's will. Although our natural capacity to choose is warped, now "every child of God *can* obey him" (1 John 5:4).

And somehow we sense it. We know a person who

claims to be a Christian, but who's under a dominance of the old laws can't be for real. Actually, such a Christian can't even be a for-real person. A for-real person seems to be what he *is*. And a Christian *is* someone new and different.

Free from pressures?

Many think we should be free from pressures. A young California girl writes:

> I thought my girl friend had gone all the way in becoming a Christian. Well, the night we got home she called her mother from my home. Her mother and father were split (her father left). She told me she hated God and religion and anything to do with Him. She thought God was going to make her life a "paradise." The things she said to me finally made me break up (cry). My mother started screaming and yelling at me when I asked her for help. She wouldn't understand.

Life a paradise for a Christian? Many expect it, but it doesn't work out that way. Other people still disappoint us. Hopes are still dashed. Moms and dads divorce. And the pressures aren't just from outside. Many a person who has "gone all the way in becoming a Christian" still struggles with doubt and fear and hate inside. Yes, even hate.

Why? Why all the old feelings if what's inside is new? Why do they continue if we've got a new set of capacities and desires that make what's "natural" now harmonize with God?

You've probably not only heard the answer—no doubt you've experienced it. We're pulled *two* ways from inside. Here's how the Bible puts it: "We natually love to do evil things that are just the opposite of the things that the Holy Spirit tells us to do; and the good things we want to

do when the Spirit has his way with us are just the opposite of our natural desires. These two forces within us are
constantly fighting each other to win control over us and
our wishes are never free from their pressures" (Gal.
5:17).

With these two complete and contrary natures now a
part of our personality, there comes a shift in battlefields.
A for-real person experiences a battle between his natural
inclinations and his standards. A non-Christian "wins"
this battle when he succeeds in governing his life by his
standards. No one, of course, *completely* wins. All fall
short, even when outwardly conforming. As we've seen,
the evil in us intrudes in some way. But conduct is the
battlefield.

This is never the battlefield for someone trying to live as
a for-real Christian. For him the battlefield has shifted
inside. The way is between his ever-present evil inclinations and the inclinations that were implanted as new life
from God.

This is why the Bible doesn't say that the fruit of God's
work in us is acts, such as witnessing, praying, being
kind. The fruit, the Bible says, is "love, joy, peace, pa-
tience, kindness, goodness, faithfulness, gentleness,
self-control" (Gal. 5:22 RSV). *The mark of reality is inside!*

Recall Carl? He did the right things. He went to church.
He had devotions, prayed, obeyed his parents. How
about him? Well, let's say that one night Carl's dad, after
promising him the car, said, "Carl, I've got to have the car
tonight myself. Sorry, but you'll just have to take it
another time." How might Carl feel? Disappointed? Resentful? Even angry?

Carl, as a for-real person who lives by his standards,
might well swallow his disappointment and say, "OK,
Dad. I know you wouldn't do it if you didn't have to."

Would he be living up to his standards as a for-real person? Surely. But *if he's still angry and resentful inside, he
hasn't made it as a for-real Christian!* To be for real, a
Christian's actions have to do more than fit standards.
They have to flow from the heart.

It's at this point that what we said earlier about being a
for-real person and being a for-real Christian come together. He chooses to submit to parents because this is
right, even when what's inside cries out to rebel. He
chooses to reject the pull of the crowd and live in his own,
even though what's inside fights desperately against
his choice. A for-real Christian submits too. A for-real
Christian rejects popularity for its own sake too. But a
for-real Christian *wants* to. For him it's not a fight of de-

sires against his standards, it's an eager desire to live the life his standards describe. His inner self and his biblical standards are in perfect harmony.

So we see the significance of Carl's words, the ones we quoted earlier: "Now I delight in doing the things I used to do." He has the mark of reality inside.

Lost in the shuffle

Last chapter we suggested that biblical standards can't help us find this reality. The Ten Commandments can't touch what's inside us. In this chapter we've seen that God's strategy is to work inside us, not to change what's there but to implant something new. Now within us is a nature that is the same as God's, one that spontaneously does what is good and right. The Bible says we've "become partakers of the divine nature" (2 Peter 1:4 RSV). The question is no longer one of conformity to standards. It becomes one of dominance. Which nature is going to be in control?

Since the battlefield has shifted inside, standards—which come from *outside*—seem to have been lost in the shuffle! And this raises a question. What place do biblical standards have in living a for-real Christian life?

The answer may shock you. It's the one word. *None!* The Christian life has to be the spontaneous overflow of the life God has planted within us. Our task isn't to conform, it's to let Christ transform.

This does not mean giving free rein to every impulse we feel. The Bible talks much about those who advocate this. Peter writes:

> These very teachers who offer this "freedom" . . . are themselves slaves to sin and destruction. For a man is a slave to whatever controls him. And when a person has escaped from the wicked ways of the world by learning

about our Lord and Saviour Jesus Christ, and then gets tangled up with sin and becomes its slave again, he is worse off then he was before" (2 Peter 2:19-20).

Never forget a Christian has *two* sets of impulses bursting inside him. Just "letting go" neglects this fact and fails to recognize the power of the old. It's often hard to be really sure which nature is the source of our conscious desires.

Then, don't we need standards after all? Yes, we do, in the sense that biblical standards are an expression of God's character and thus a good mirror before which to place our own impulses. God's standards will show up sin for what it is. But these standards will never give the new nature the power to dominate. They never bring us to victory.

"You have been given freedom," the Bible says, "not freedom to do wrong, but freedom to love and serve each other" (Gal. 5:13). This is not a life of forced conformity. This is life flowing as spontaneous love from within. And this is what it takes to be a for-real Christian.

What happens next?

When standards lose place as a dominant factor in the Christian life, the priority of other truths is reestablished. When this happens in your thinking, you'll be much further ahead in living a for-real Christian life. What ought you to understand about this point?

Christian living takes a Christian. Christianity *isn't* just a way of looking at life. It isn't just a sincere attempt to live by Christian standards, or to pattern one's life after Christ. A Christian is a person in whom God has implanted a new life, His own life.

Many other things are involved when a person becomes a Christian. Forgiveness of sins is what we hear of most often. But in each case, *God acts.* He enters our lives and changes us. And it's only when God changes us that we can have a change in our experience.

In the Bible commitment to Christ is called faith. "Faith" doesn't mean to "just decide to believe one way." "You can never please God without faith," the Bible says, "without depending on him" (Heb. 11:6). That's what God wants from us, dependence on Him. How do we begin? We begin with what He says. "Christ died for our sins" (1 Cor. 15:3) is His message. "God so loved the world that he gave his only Son, that whoever believes in him should not perish but have eternal life" (John 3:16 RSV) is His word. This is where depending on God begins. At the cross.

A Christian is both sinner and saint. Several studies have shown that Christian teens tend to assume older Christians have "arrived." Really, no one arrives. The old nature is always there. It's always active, pushing into our thoughts, always trying to warp our actions and our lives. It always attempts to force us back into old patterns of life.

In a way, this dual nature of ours helps make the Christian life an adventure. Every day becomes an opportunity to see the new life bubbling up within us, expressing itself in all we think and do. As with any true adventure, there's an ever-present element of danger. Unless we're on our toes, living alertly, we can slip back and live by the old. So the challenge is always there. This kind of life can't be boiled down into codes, and starched stiffly into routine patterns of acceptable behavior. It must be fresh every day, a new challenge, a new adventure. This life can never be a drag.

The Christian can't go it alone. It's hard enough to try living by standards. If you shift your focus from behavior to motive, to the very impulses that you adopt standards in order to curb, you begin to feel helpless.

Often new Christians, with their new natures, feel a little more confident. But try to go it alone and see what happens. Next time dad refuses the car, look inside and see what feelings well up. Next time mom says, "Can't you *ever* keep your room straight!" look inside, and see what's there. Next time you hear of a cutting remark made about you by a friend, look inside. What's there? Which nature is expressing itself?

That's what's so disturbing. We want to live that new and different life. But wanting doesn't make it so. When we try to live it on our own, life loses that spirit of adventure and becomes a dreary series of defeats. Life falls into patterns and forms, losing the spontaneity of the reality Christ promises.

Even a true Christian, one with that new life from God, can't go it alone. It takes Someone else to turn that new life on and make our lives overflow.

We've got the capacity. Now all we need is the power.

Steps to take

1. Do you have the mark of reality inside you? If not, check what you think is the reason.

    ☐ I'm not a Christian, and have only the old nature.

    ☐ I believe I have both natures, but can't get the new one in charge.

2. If you checked the first box, study Romans 5:6-11. Will you have confidence in God to do what He says here? If so, tell Him.

3. If you checked the second box, reread the chapter carefully. Jot down any reasons you discover that help explain why you have trouble.

10

The open secret

When we talk to teens who claim to have the mark of reality inside, one theme keeps popping up. See if you can discover it in these thoughtful paragraphs from three young people.

First, let's hear again from Carl, the fellow in the last two chapters. He writes,

> What has been a joy to me is to see that God loves me as a Father, that He is concerned about my growing up, that He is working in my life by His Spirit in ways I don't dream of. I think it could be said that God expects from us primarily our trust in His ability to save us and cause us to grow up. As we search the Word of God and see the expression of His Person, and as we trustingly allow Him to work, the growth we are so eager for will follow as a result of His working. I have come to expect less and less of myself and trust Him more.

An Iowa girl shares similar feelings.

> When I was a senior in high school I became terribly depressed; I couldn't quite make out the why of life. Usually I am a very happy person, but I got to the point where

happiness seemed a never never thing I'd outgrown.
About that time I heard a short devotional. It was on Psalm
37:4, "Delight thyself in the Lord and he will give you the
desires of your heart." I was desperate enough to try anything, so the next two Sundays I spent quietly, no
homework, "not seeking my own pleasure," no T.V., devotions in the afternoon. The desire of my heart was to be
happy and content. The Lord gave it to me, showing how
wonderfully He keeps His promises. If we seek Him we
even have what we DESIRE, not just what we need! Of
course, if we are seeking Him our desires will be in tune
with His will.

A North Dakota boy adds his experience.

As a freshman this year in Wheaton College, I constantly
worried about flunking out of college, and if I was in the
Lord's will. In a devotional period in one of my classes, the
teacher was telling if we commit our problems to the Lord,
He will take care of them. I claimed the verse in Proverbs
3:5-6. "Trust in the Lord with all thy heart and lean not
unto thine own understanding, in all thy ways acknowl-
edge him and he shall direct thy paths." Well, the Lord
answered my prayer and now I sleep well and am doing
better in my classes and am now a more stable Christian.
He has also taught me that I have to do my part, and then
He'll give me the strength to do what He wants.

Look back over each of these, and you'll note that not
one is talking about standards. Not one is talking about
his convictions. Each talks instead about experiencing the
Lord as a real person. "I've only been a Christian a little
over a year," says an eighteen-year-old from New Jersey,
"and Christianity is still fresh and vital to me—because
Christ is real and vital." This is the secret—a real and vital
relationship with Jesus Christ.

A solution to offer

What he says is true. Christianity as doctrines, as

standards, as convictions pressed on us from others, is both dead and deadening. Christianity as a personal commitment to Jesus Christ is vital and alive.

Sometimes it's hard to understand how this open secret of Christianity is so easily overlooked. Certainly the place of our personal relationship with God dominates the thought of the New Testament. The Apostle Paul didn't leave Judaism because Christianity offered a better or more rational system. He left his high rank and considered it "worthless when compared with the priceless gain of knowing Christ Jesus my Lord. I have put aside all else," he says in Philippians, "counting it worth less than nothing, in order that I can have Christ. . . . I have given up everything else . . . [that I may] really know Christ and experience the mighty power that brought him back to life again" (Phil. 3:8, 10). When Paul prayed for people, he didn't ask God to help them keep standards. He asked God to help them know Christ. "I pray that Christ will be more and more at home in your hearts, living within you as you trust in him. May your roots go down deep into the soil of God's marvelous love; and may you be able to feel and understand, . . . and to experience this love for yourselves" (Eph. 3:17, 19).

This is the answer we have to give when people ask how to let God live His life in them. "Just as you trusted Christ to save you," says the Bible, "trust him too for each day's problems; live in vital union with him" (Col. 2:6-7). The answer to *How?* is found in your personal relationship to Jesus Christ. And the reason for this is *power.*

Look at it this way. You may have a car loaded with horsepower. But it won't run without gas. You may have a potent new nature, but it won't run without a source of power either. And that source of power is God, and God alone.

Often it's hard for a person to view his relationship with Christ as the answer to inner struggle. Each of us still tends to grasp at standards, and insist on the chance to *do* something. There is much that we *can* do to grow as Christians. But there's nothing we can do to "fuel" the new nature. Nothing at all. "Everyone can see," says Paul, who knew how deceitful his old nature was, "that the glorious power within us must be from God and is not our own" (2 Cor. 4:7).

That's something we can't get around. If a change is to be made inside, the power must be from God.

When we focus on our relationship with Christ as the central issue in our Christian lives, it completely reverses our approach to the Bible.

Many people come to the Bible to find standards and rules (or to justify theirs!). This is a dreadfully dangerous approach to Scripture. Why? Let's go back to power. If God powers the new nature, what powers the old? What energizes it, stirs it up, gets it in motion? Strange as it seems, the answer is *standards!* "Our sinful passions," says the Bible, are "aroused [literally, energized] by the law" (Rom. 7:5 RSV). When we try to impose standards on our old nature, we merely stir it up!

Take, for instance, a situation in your own life where a rule is imposed. Say that for some reason dad says, "No car for two weeks," or "No phone privileges for you, young lady." What do you almost automatically *want* to do? Why, you want to use the car, or you want to use the phone. Because you're told you *can't* do it, your desire is heightened. That's what happens inside, when we view a biblical command as a code or law. That which is inside is stirred up to want the opposite!

This is why it's dangerous to search the Bible for standards. "The power of sin is the law," the Bible says (1 Cor. 15:56 RSV), and that is exactly what it means. Even God's law can't help us control what's inside. Even God's law will only increase the pressures of the old nature.

How then should we approach the Bible? Carl said it: "We search the Word of God and see the expression of His Person." The Bible is the place where we meet Christ.

To develop a personal relationship with anyone there has to be communication—talk, back and forth. As you openly and freely share your ideas and feelings and desires, a person comes to know you. And as the other shares his ideas, his feelings and his desires, you come to know him. Without this kind of communication, no personal relationship can grow. This truth points us to the role of the Bible in the Christian life.

Open sharing by us is vital and necessary in our relationship with God. A twenty-year-old Illinois fellow said:

> I went through a period in high school when I doubted God's love and concern. I remember going to church just to keep up a good front, but after a while my cold shoulder toward God began to bother me. I soon realized that I was cheating myself by ignoring my only source of help. I then asked God to forgive me and to restore our fellowship and friendship to what it had been before. At first these requests just seemed to hit the ceiling and bounce right back, but when I finally admitted my doubts and sins to God, the communication line opened.

Openness is always what God wants. "I felt guilty for doubting," says a Michigan boy, "so I tried to repress them, but in the pinch they always came up again. It wasn't until I aired them completely and sincerely that peace returned and effectiveness with it."

But such sharing has to be two-way! *We have to listen as Christ shares Himself with us. And He does this in the Bible.* If we come to the Word to meet God—not just to discover rules of life or to erect doctrinal structures—He speaks to us. He shares His thoughts, He shares Himself. No wonder so many writers and speakers call the Bible "God's love letter." It is. And as we see Him in the Word, our love is quickened too.

The peculiar power of love

We see it often in a young couple. At home she hated to keep her room clean, and was quick to snap back when mom insisted she take the vacuum and go to work. Now she's married. Instead of one room to care for, she's got their whole apartment. But, amazingly, she throws herself into it. She decorates, polishes, hangs curtains and keeps her house attractive and clean. Why? She's doing it for *him.* Somehow love has changed the nature of her tasks. Now she wants to do what mom could hardly make her do before.

This is what happens in our lives when we love Christ. Carl put it, "Now I delight to do the things I used to do." The Bible says it this way: "Loving God means doing what he tells us to, and really that isn't hard at all" (1 John 5:3). There's a tremendous difference between looking on biblical commands as standards we have to obey, and seeing them as expressions of Christ's will which we also want.

This helps us clarify two questions about standards raised in earlier chapters.

Why doesn't a Christian need standards? It's not only that "standards" change their character. There's a deeper reason. When we love God He "turns on" the new nature, and the life that spontaneously flows from us actually

meets all the standards! The Bible says it this way: "God
. . . sending his own Son . . . condemned sin in the flesh,
in order that the just requirement of the law might be
fulfilled in us, who walk not according to the flesh but
according to the Spirit" (Rom. 8:3-4 RSV).

When you think about it, this isn't hard to understand.
Where did biblical standards come from? From God, as an
expression of His character. Where does our new nature
come from? From God, as His own life implanted in us.
"Christ *in you,*" Paul calls it, the "hope of all the glorious
things to come" (Col. 1:27 *Phillips*). Of course this life
matches the standards—both spring from the same
source!

This is why a Christian just can't choose standards that
are contrary to Scripture and still be for real. No one can
say he's living God's life, and be out of harmony with
God's Word. "If anyone says, 'I love God,' " the Bible
says, "but keeps on hating his brother, he is a liar"
(1 John 4:20). The life of God is always in harmony with
the Word of God.

The crucial issue in the Christian's life, then, is not
conforming to standards, but his relationship with Jesus
Christ. When we live spontaneously for Him, we need no
standards.

But there's a second problem. *How can we know just
what He wants us to do?* It's a little too simple to say, "Just
read your Bible."

Remember chapter 7? There we saw Carol had trouble
trying to *apply* biblical guidelines to discover what God
wanted her to do. Should she be a cheerleader or not?
True, the Bible tells us many things that are always God's
will. "Have nothing to do with sexual sin, impurity, lust
and shameful desires" (Col. 3:5) is, for example, a sharp
and clear expression of what God wants. But take the

person who, like Carol, is trying to decide if he should build a friendship with a specific unsaved individual or group. He can find biblical principles that seem to encourage such involvement, and others that warn against it. What does God want him to do in *this particular situation?*

Often we make a mistake at this point. We search out biblical principles and reduce them to rules. But Christianity isn't lived by rules and laws! It is life lived spontaneously, looking to Christ for direction, not to a formalized code. You simply cannot decide that "a Christian must become involved with the unsaved," or that "a Christian must never become involved with the unsaved," and then fit your life into that pattern. At times Christ will want you to become involved. At times He'll want you *not* to form certain friendships. You must be responsive to *Him.*

Actually, this is what Carol decided. She would go to tryouts and expect God to close the door if He wished. And He did. The important thing is that *Carol counted on Christ to act as a person.*

Knowing Christ as a person changes things. A person is free to act in a way that a rule cannot. The Bible is God's Word, but it is *not* a set of rules. It is God, talking over the complexities of life, sharing His views, the way He thinks, the way He is. And as we meet Him there, as we come to know Him better, we'll understand better the ways His life can be lived through us. But no matter how well we know the Bible, we can only choose His will as He speaks to us in each situation. We must count on Him to act as a person.

That's another exciting thing about the Christian life. Christ speaks to us. He guides us each day. Some days He may show us His will as He did Carol, by shutting a door.

Other days He may guide us through a friend, or through a book. Or He may bring to mind something we've read in His Word. When we know Him well, when we meet Him daily and listen to Him speak to us through His Word, we come to know His voice.

How this changes life! When you're living daily with Christ, life loses its vast fearsomeness and becomes that bright adventure we mentioned in the last chapter. How tragic that so few youth today find life an adventure. "Most Lutheran teenagers," wrote Gordon Smedsrud,[1] after a survey of thousands of Missouri Synod high schoolers, "do not have this kind of inner fortress and boldness of faith. They are timid and unsure of themselves, afraid of making mistakes. They lack self-confidence because they lack confidence in Christ."

But this is what the Christian life boils down to! Confidence in Christ. For Christ is a living Person who desires to live close to you.

This is the open secret of your faith.

A for-real Christian life

Being a for-real Christian does challenge; it does demand determination, even for a great Christian like the Apostle Paul. "Whatever it takes," he wrote, almost grimly, "I will be one who lives in the fresh newness of life of those who are alive from the dead" (Phil. 3:11).

But what *can* it take if Christ does it all? What is our part?

Cultivate your relationship with Christ. You don't grow closer to any person by ignoring him! To live close to Christ, to find His life spilling over into your experience, to become sensitive to His will—this is the heart of Christian living. There can be no reality in your Christian experience apart from Him.

So you *must* spend time with Him, both talking and listening. "Pray about everything," the Bible says, "tell God your needs and don't forget to thank Him for His answers. If you do this you will know God's peace, which is far more wonderful than the human mind can understand" (Phil. 4:6-7). And as you seek Christ in the Word and listen to Him, your roots will "grow down into him and draw up nourishment from him" (Col. 2:7a).

"See that you go on growing in the Lord" (Col. 2:7b), the Bible says. This isn't just offhand advice. This is crucial. This is what it takes to "become strong and vigorous in the truth" (Col. 2:7b). This is what it takes to become a for-real Christian.

Commit your life to Christ. Sometimes people take their relationship with Christ for granted. He's just Someone who tags along until we need Him. But that's turning the relationship upside down. *He* is God, we aren't!

Some have become so concerned about this attitude that they've taught that to be a Christian a person has to accept Christ as Lord, as well as have confidence in Him as Saviour. This really isn't true. But it is true that getting your relationship to Christ in perspective is necessary for reality in your Christian life. *He's got to be in charge, not you!*

This is what Paul writes to the Christians at Rome. "I plead with you to give your bodies to God. Let them be a living sacrifice, holy—the kind he can accept. When you think of what he has done for you, is this too much to ask? . . . Then you will learn from your own experience how his ways will really satisfy you!" (Rom. 12:1-2).

It's only then, when you've committed your life and your will completely to Christ, that you can become that "new and different person with a fresh newness in all you do and think" (Rom. 12:2).

Be responsive to Christ. The "I do's" of a wedding ceremony never need to be repeated, but each day of married life must be a working out of the initial commitment. Committing ourselves to Christ as Lord is like this. When you present yourself to Him, He accepts you. Now you need only work out your commitment daily.

How do you do this? By being responsive. The Bible presents the sure pathway to loving and knowing Christ better. "Those who do what Christ tells them," it says, "will learn to love God more and more" (1 John 2:5). Usually this is what's wrong when a young person complains that his devotional life is meaningless, or that Christ just doesn't seem real. Christ will grow real, you'll love Him more and more, but only as you respond to Him. And responding to Him means doing what He wants, doing what He tells us.

This doesn't mean reading the Bible for rules and laws. But it doesn't mean reading the Bible just for information either. Remember that Christ is speaking to you in the Bible. He's sharing His thoughts, His feelings, His desires, and the way He looks at life. Each day, as you read His Word, look for these. Test your own daily life against what you discover of His will. Then, as He talks to you, jot down specific ways you can respond during that day. And do it.

This is the only way to know Christ better. And it's only "as you know him better" that "he will give you, through his great power, everything you need for living a truly good life" (2 Peter 1:3).

Look expectantly to Christ. Count on God to work in *your* life daily. Carl said it: "I think that God expects from us primarily our trust in His ability to save us and cause us to grow up." He has learned the open secret. God is at work in us and through us, and our part is simply to trust.

This is true even when we feel weak, and unable to respond. "I am with you," God promises, "and that is all you need. My power shows up best in weak people" (2 Cor. 12:9).

With this promise we can make life an adventure. We can confidently face each day, sure that whatever it holds, God will be with us, working out His plan for us, causing our lives to overflow with His presence. With this promise, knowing Christ intimately as a person who cares for us, we can live by faith.

"What is faith?" the Bible asks. "It is the confident assurance that something we want is going to happen. It is the certainty that what we hope for is waiting for us, even though we cannot see it up ahead" (Heb. 11:1). And this—life with zest and adventure and full of confidence in God—is living the Christian life "for real."

Steps to take

Look over the four suggestions on pp. 122-24. What steps do *you* need to take toward reality? You can take them! It's your choice.

Notes

Chapter 1

[1]Milton Strommen, *Profiles of Church Youth* (St. Louis: Concordia, 1962), p. 237.

Chapter 5

[1]Earnest A. Smith, *American Youth Culture* (New York: Free Press of Glencoe, 1962), p. 18.
[2]Albert Pikunas, *Psychology of Human Development* (New York: McGraw-Hill, 1964), p. 22.

Chapter 8

[1]Graham T. Blaine, *Youth and the Hazards of Affluence* (New York: Harper & Row, 1966), p. 122.
[2]Paul Tournier, *The Person Reborn* (New York: Harper & Row, 1966).

Chapter 10

[1]Gordon Smedsrud, *What Youth Are Thinking* (Minneapolis: Augsburg, 1960), p. 22.